José Orlandis
A SHORT HISTORY OF THE CATHOLIC
CHURCH

*José Orlandis was born in Palma de Mallorca in
1918. For twenty-five years he held the chair of
history of law at the University of Saragossa.
Sometime director of the Institute of Church History
at the University of Navarre, he is the author of
many books, particularly in the field of church
history.*

A short history
of the catholic Church

JOSE ORLANDIS

FOUR COURTS PRESS

This translation by Michael Adams of *Historia breve del Cristianismo*
(Ediciones Rialp, S.A. Madrid, 1983) is published by
Four Courts Press Limited, Fumbally Lane, Dublin 8.
Email: info@four-courts-press.ie
The 1993 edition includes additions by the author.

First edition 1985
Second English edition 1993, reprinted 1998

Printed in Great Britain by
The Guernsey Press Co. Ltd, Guernsey, Channel Islands

Contents

Preface

The history of the catholic Church is naturally of interest to a catholic reader; but it should be of interest to any educated person for the simple reason that it is part and parcel of the history of mankind over the last two thousand years: our civilization has largely been shaped over that period, which has earned the title of 'the Christian era.' I have written this book for both Christians and non-Christians, and I have quite properly called it a 'short' history. But the fact that it is short does not mean that it leaves out important things or that it only skims the surface. I have made it short in order to make it accessible to a wide readership, to people who might not be inclined to read a more elaborate book. Therefore, I have tried to combine simplicity and depth, leaving numerous questions to one side in an attempt to follow what I consider to be the main thread of Christian history.

The book is divided into thirty-five chapters, each headed with a short summary indicating the main subjects dealt with. This *Short history of the catholic Church* is primarily a book of religious history, but I have tried always to bear in mind the political, cultural and social features of the times in which Christians were living. The chronological table at the end of the book may help readers to position Christian events in their historical context.

Every book is written with a particular purpose; what I have tried to do here is quite simple, but that is not to say it is not ambitious: I would hope that the man in the street, after reading this book, would have a fairly good grasp of what happened over the first twenty centuries of the history of Christianity.

JOSE ORLANDIS

1

The Origins of Christianity

Christianity is the religion founded by Jesus Christ, the Son of God become man. People became Christians — disciples of Christ — through baptism, thereby entering the visible community of salvation which is called the Church.

1. By Christianity we mean the religion founded by Jesus Christ, the Son of God become man. Jesus himself and his teachings are the bases on which the Christian religion rests. Christians look to Jesus Christ as their redeemer and teacher: they recognize him as their God and lord and they hold to his teaching.

2. At a precise moment in history and in a particular place on earth, the Son of God became man and made his appearance in human history. Jesus' place of birth was Bethlehem, in Judea; he was born when Herod the Great was king of Judea and Quirinius was governor of Syria, in the reign of Caesar Augustus, emperor of Rome (cf. Mt 2:1; Lk 2:1-2). Christ lived on earth until another documented moment in time: his passion, death and resurrection took place in Jerusalem, starting on the fourteenth day of Nisan in the year 30. At that time Caiaphas held the position of high priest, the procurator Pontius Pilate ruled Judea and Tiberius was emperor of Rome.

3. Jesus put himself forward as the Christ, the messiah foretold by the prophets and eagerly expected by the people of Israel. In Caesarea Philippi, against the background of various opinions as to who he was, Jesus asked his Apostles: 'But who do you say that I am?' Peter replied very emphatically: 'You are the Christ, the Son of the living God.' Jesus accepted this description of himself and confirmed it quite unequivocally: '. . . [for] flesh and blood has not revealed this to you, but my Father who is in heaven' (cf. Mt 16:13-17). On the night of his passion, before the chief priests and all the Sanhedrin, he openly declared that he was the Son of God, the messiah. In response to the solemn question put to him by the chief priest, the supreme religious authority in Israel, 'Are you the Christ, the Son of the Blessed?', Jesus said 'I am' (Mk 14:61-62).

4. 'He came to his own home, and his own people received him not' (Jn 1: 11). These words of the first chapter of St John's Gospel report the drama of the rejection of the Saviour by the chosen people. At this time most Jews had a political-nationalistic idea of what the messiah would be like: they expected him to be a kind of earthly leader who would free their nation from the oppressive yoke of the Romans and restore the kingdom of Israel in all its splendour. Jesus did not fit this image, for his kingdom was not of this world (cf. Jn 18:36). Therefore, they failed to recognize him; instead, he was rejected by the leaders of the people and condemned to death by crucifixion.

5. The miracles Jesus performed during his public life were the proof he offered of his messiahship and his way of demonstrating the truth of his teachings. His miracles and teachings, combined with Jesus' unique personality, were what caused people to become his disciples, the first of whom were the twelve Apostles. Initially, their commitment was defective: for they shared many of their contemporaries' prejudices; they found it difficult to grasp exactly what Jesus' redemptive mission was — which explains how terribly disconcerted they were by his passion and death.

6. The resurrection of Jesus is the central dogma of Christianity and is the decisive proof of the truth of his teaching. 'If Christ has not been raised,' St Paul wrote, 'then our preaching is in vain and your faith is in vain' (1 Cor 15:14). The fact of the resurrection (nothing was further from the thoughts of the Apostles and disciples) was thrust on them by the sheer force of evidence: 'But in fact Christ has been raised from the dead, the first fruits of those who have fallen asleep' (1 Cor 15:20; cf. Lk 24:27-44; Jn 20:24-28). From then on, the Apostles put themselves forward as 'witnesses' of the risen Jesus (cf. Acts 2:22; 3:15), reporting his resurrection to the whole world and sealing their testimony with their own blood. The disciples of Jesus Christ recognized his divinity; they believed that his death was responsible for their redemption and that they had received the fullness of revelation, transmitted to them by the Master and gathered up in the form of scripture and tradition.

7. But Jesus Christ not only founded a religion — Christianity;

he established a Church. The Church — the new people of God — was established in the form of a visible community of salvation which people join through baptism. The Church was grounded on the Apostle Peter, to whom Christ promised the primacy — 'and on this rock I will build my Church' (Mt 16:18); Christ confirmed this after his resurrection and conferred this responsibility on Peter: 'Feed my lambs,' 'Tend my sheep' (cf. Jn 21:15-17). The Church of Jesus Christ will last until the end of time, as long as the world lasts and there are men on earth: 'and the gates of hell shall not prevail against it' (Mt 16:18) The final stage in the establishment of the Church occurred on the day of Pentecost, which is when its history begins.

2

The Synagogue and the Church

Persecuted by the Sanhedrin, the Christians very soon parted company with the Synagogue. From the very beginning, Christianity was universal, that is, open to the Gentiles, to whom the rules of the Mosaic law did not apply.

1. 'A disciple is not above his teacher' (Mt 10:24), Jesus told his disciples. The Sanhedrin declared Jesus a criminal to be punished by death for claiming to be the messiah, the Son of God. It was only logical for the Jewish authorities to be hostile to his Apostles, when they proclaimed that Jesus was risen and confirmed their preaching by various public miracles. The Sanhedrin tried to silence them, but Peter replied to the high priest, 'we must obey God rather than man' (Acts 5:29). The Apostles were put under the lash, but neither threats nor violence could silence them, and they left rejoicing 'that they were counted worthy to suffer dishonour' for the name of Jesus. The death by stoning of St Stephen the deacon marked the beginning of severe persecution of Jesus' disciples. The cleavage between Christianity and Judaism grew steadily deeper and more overt.

2. In contrast with the national character of the Jewish religion, the universalism of Christianity soon expressed itself. Disciples of Jesus, in flight from Jerusalem, reached Antioch in Syria, one of the great cities of the east. Some of them were Hellenists, with an outlook more open than that of Palestinian Jews, and they began to proclaim the gospel to the Gentiles. In cosmopolitan Antioch, the universalism of the Church became patent; and it was there, for the first time, that Christ's followers were called Christians.

3. The universality of the redemption and of the Church of Jesus Christ was formally confirmed by a miraculous event in which the Apostle Peter was the protagonist. The extraordinary signs surrounding the conversion of Cornelius, a centurion at Caesarea, and his family, cleared up any doubts Peter had on this subject; as he put it, 'Truly I perceive that God shows no particularity, but in every nation anyone who fears him and does what is right is acceptable to him' (Acts 10:34-35). The news that Peter had given baptism to uncircumcised Gentiles caused consternation in Jerusalem. Peter had to report his experience in great detail before the Jewish Christians in this holy city changed their minds and shed their deeply rooted prejudices. They began to realize that the redemption brought by Christ was universal: the Church was open to everyone: 'When they heard this they were silenced. And they glorified God, saying, "Then to the Gentiles also God has granted repentance unto life" ' (Acts 11:18).

4. But one last obstacle remained before Christian universalism won the day. It was difficult for many Jewish Christians, attached as they were to their old traditions, to understand how Gentiles could be members of the Church. They felt that for Gentile converts to have access to salvation they needed at the very least to be circumcised and to keep the regulations of the law of Moses. This naturally disturbed Christians of Gentile background, so the Church was forced to examine the whole question of the relationship between the old law and the new law, and to affirm unequivocally the Church's independence of the Synagogue.

5. To discuss these fundamental problems the so-called 'council' of Jerusalem met in the year 49. At this assembly Paul and Barnabas spoke on behalf of the churches of Gentile background and bore witness to the wonders God had worked among them. Peter once again spoke with authority in favour of Christians' freedom vis-à-vis Jewish legal observances. On the proposal of James, bishop of Jerusalem, the council agreed not to lay any unnecessary burdens on Gentile converts: they should only have to obey a few simple rules: keep away from fornication and, as regard the old law, abstain from meat which was strangled or had been sacrificed to idols (Acts 15:1-33), thus definitively solving the problem of the relationships between Christianity and Judaism. Jewish Christians in Palestine still followed their own style for a while, but they were a minority within a Christian Church ever more widespread throughout the Gentile world.

6. The great promoters of the spread of Christianity were the Apostles, acting in obedience to Christ's commandment to proclaim the gospel to all the nations. Due to lack of historical documents it is difficult to find out much about the missionary activity of most of the Apostles. We do know that the Apostle Peter, on leaving Palestine, made Antioch his base (there was an important Christian community there already). It is possible that he also lived for a time in Corinth, but his final base was Rome, the capital of the empire; he was the first bishop of the Roman church. In Rome he underwent martyrdom in the persecution unleashed by Emperor Nero (*c.* 64). John the Apostle, after staying a long time in Palestine, moved to Ephesus, where he lived for very many years, so much so that the churches of Asia regarded him as their own Apostle. Very early traditions speak of apostolic activities of James the Greater in Spain, of Thomas in India, of Mark the Evangelist in Alexandria, etc.

7. Information about the apostolic activity of St Paul is by far the most extensive, thanks to the accounts in the Acts of the Apostles and the important corpus of Pauline letters. St Paul was the Apostle of the Gentiles, *par excellence*, and his missionary journeys brought the gospel to Asia Minor and Greece, where he founded and directed many churches. Taken prisoner in Jerusalem, his long captivity gave him an opportunity to bear witness to Christ before the Sanhedrin, the Roman governors of Judea and King Agrippa II. After being brought to Rome he was set free by Caesar's courts and probably during this period made a missionary journey to Spain, which he had been planning for some time. Imprisoned for a second time, he was tried again and found guilty and died a martyr in the imperial city.

8. The work of the Apostles does not complete the picture of the spread of Christianity in the ancient world. For the most part, the bearers of the first tidings of the gospel must have been ordinary, humble people — civil servants, businessmen, soldiers and slaves. As a generalization, it may be said that during these early centuries Christianity was to be found more in the cities than among the rural communities. By the time the Church obtained its freedom, in the fourth century, Christianity was deeply rooted in many parts of the near east, such as Syria, Asia Minor and Armenia; and in the west, in Rome and its surrounding area and in Latin Africa. The gospel also had a considerable presence in the Nile valley and in various parts of Italy, Spain and Gaul.

3

Christianity and the Pagan Empire

Christianity began and developed within the political and cultural framework of the Roman empire. For three centuries, the pagan empire persecuted the Christians because their religion represented a 'rival' form of universalism and forbade its adherents to offer religious worship to the emperor.

1. The birth and early development of Christianity took place with the political and cultural framework of the Roman empire. It is true that pagan Rome persecuted the Christians for three centuries; but it would be wrong to see the empire as only a negative factor in the spread of the gospel. The fact that Rome had imposed unity on the Greco-Latin world meant that over a huge area, under a single supreme authority, peace and order reigned. This situation lasted until well into the third century and good communications among the various parts of the empire made it easy for ideas to circulate. The Roman roads and the sea-routes of the Mediterranean provided channels for the good news of Christianity to spread over the whole Mediterranean area.

2. A common language — based on Greek, at first, and on Greek and Latin, later — made it easier for people to communicate and understand one another. Paganism was in crisis, very many spiritually sensitive people were searching for religious truth and were predisposed to the gospel. These factors, undoubtedly favoured the spread of Christianity.

3. But there were also very serious obstacles in the way of people embracing the Christian faith. For Christians of Jewish background it meant breaking with their community of origin — which now regarded them as deserters and traitors. Gentile converts, especially those belonging to the upper classes, encountered similar difficulties: their faith did not allow them take part in a series of traditional pagan-religious practices involving worship of Rome and the emperor, yet these practices were part and parcel of a citizen's everyday life and they were a conventional sign of loyalty to the empire. Hence the accusation so often levelled against the Christians that they were 'atheists.' This was a reason why they were threatened with persecution and martyrdom — a threat which hung over them for centuries and meant that to become a Christian involved taking risks; and demanded a high degree of moral courage.

4. What caused the great confrontation between the pagan empire and Christianity? The Christian religion encouraged people to respect and obey lawful authority. 'Render to Caesar the things that are Caesar's, and to God the things that are God's' (cf. Mt 22:15-21) was the principle given by Christ himself. The Apostles developed this teaching: 'Let every person be subject to the governing authorities. For there is no authority except God' (Rom 13:1), wrote St Paul to the faithful at Rome; and St Peter exhorted the disciples to 'Fear God. Honour the emperor' (1 Pet 2:17). The empire, for its part, was liberal in religious matters and easily tolerated new forms of worship and foreign divinities. The collision and the break occurred because Rome tried to get its Christian subjects to do something they could not do — render it the religious homage of adoration which may be given lawfully to God alone.

5. The circumstances surrounding the first persecution — Nero's — had enormous effects, despite the fact that this persecution does not seem to have extended further than the city of Rome. The Christians were officially accused of a heinous crime — the burning of the city — and this created a widespread public opinion hostile to the new religion. The historian Tacitus regarded Christianity as 'a pernicious superstition'; Suetonius described it as 'novel and mischievous'; Pliny the Younger as 'depraved and extravagant.' Tacitus went as far as calling the Christians enemies of mankind. Therefore it is not surprising that ordinary people attributed to Christians all sorts of monstrosities such as infanticide and cannibalism, etc. According to Tertullian 'Christians to the lions' became the obligatory catch-cry of every riot.

6. From the first century on, Christianity was regarded as an 'unlawful superstition', which meant that the mere profession of Christian belief — 'bearing the name of Christ' — was a crime. This explains why many anti-Christian acts of violence in the second century originated not so much in actions of emperors or magistrates as in popular agitation and denunciation. Consequently, persecution during this period was not a general or continuous phenomenon; the Christians sometimes enjoyed long periods of peace, without this meaning that they felt any real security under the law: at any moment they could find themselves victims of violence. The ambiguous attitude of certain second-century emperors is reflected in Trajan's famous reply when Pliny, the governor of Bithynia, consulted him on what policy he should adopt towards Christians. Trajan replied that the authorities should not take the initiative in seeking out Christians or pay any attention to anonymous informers, but that they should act whenever they received denunciations in the proper form and should condemn and execute those Christians who did not recant and who refused to sacrifice to the gods. Tertullian — a Christian apologist and a skilled lawyer — exposed the absurdity of Trajan's reply: 'If they are criminals,' he says referring to the Christians, 'why not hunt them down?; and if they are innocent, why punish them?'

7. In the third century, persecution took a different form. In the attempt to re-establish the empire after the period of 'military anarchy' — a period of serious political upheaval — part of the official policy was to restore the cult of the gods and of the emperor as a test of subjects' loyalty to Rome and its sovereign. The Christian Church came to be seen as a powerful enemy because the faithful were forbidden to engage in this form of worship. This gave rise to a new wave of persecution, this time originated by the authorities — a much more systematic persecution than theretofore.

8. The first of these great persecutions stemmed from an edict of Decius (*c.* 250) ordering all inhabitants of the empire to offer public, officially supervised sacrifice in honour of their national gods. Decius' edict took the Christians completely by surprise (Christians were now quite numerous and had become somewhat easygoing after a long period of peace). The result was that, although there were many martyrs, many not very committed Christians did offer public sacrifice or at least obtained the *libellus* stating that they had offered sacrifice; their re-integration into the Christian community later gave rise to controversies within the Church. However, the experience they underwent helped to stiffen their resolve and when, a few years later, Emperor Valerian (253-60) launched another persecution, Christian resistance was much firmer: there were many martyrs and very few Christians who proved unfaithful (these were called the *lapsi*).

9. The severest persecution was the last one, which took place at the beginning of the fourth century, in the context of the great reform of Roman institutions carried out by Emperor Diocletian. The new system of government established by the founder of the later empire was a tetrarchy — government by an 'imperial college' of four, among whom was divided the administration of the vast Roman territories. Under the tetrarchy, traditional religion was given a very important role in the regeneration of the empire, yet despite this Diocletian did not persecute the Christians during the first eighteen years of his reign. A number of factors, not least the influence of Caesar Galerius, played a part in setting off this last and worst persecution. Four edicts against Christians were promulgated between February 303 and March 304, aimed at wiping out Christianity and the Church once and for all. The persecution was violent in the extreme and made many martyrs in most provinces of the empire. Only Gaul and Britain — governed by Caesar Constantius Chlorus, who was sympathetic towards Christians and the father of the future emperor Constantine — remained practically untouched. At the end of the day the result was absolute failure. After his abdication Diocletian lived long enough to witness, from his retreat at Salonae in his native Dalmatia, the epilogue of the persecution era and the beginning of an epoch of freedom for the Church and for Christians.

4

The Life of the Early Christians

Christians formed local communities — churches — under the pastoral authority of a bishop. The bishop of Rome — the successor of the Apostle Peter — exercised a primacy over all the churches. The Eucharist was the centre of Christian life. The rejection of Gnosticism was the major doctrinal achievement of the early Church.

1. In its expansion in the ancient world Christianity adapted itself to the institutions and lifestyle of Roman society. We have already seen how the principle of Christian universalism became more and more patent; we have also looked at the relationships between the Church and the pagan empire. Now we will study the main features of life inside the Christian communities: their hierarchical and social make-up, pastoral government, discipline, liturgy, etc.

Wherever it went, classical Rome, by policy, promoted city life: municipalities and colonies developed over all the provinces of an empire in which urbanization meant Romanization. Christianity was born in this historical context, and it was in the cities that the first Christian communities established themselves, as local churches. Their surroundings were pagan and hostile — which had the effect of giving them greater internal cohesion and made for solidarity among their members. Yet these churches were not isolated nuclei: there was a real communion and communication among the churches and they all had a keen sense of being components of one and the same world-wide Church, the one and only Church founded by Jesus Christ.

2. Many of the churches of the first century were founded by Apostles, and as long as these Apostles lived they remained under their authority, being managed by a 'college' of priests who were in charge of their liturgical life and their good order. This system of government can be seen especially in the Pauline churches founded by the Apostle of the Gentiles. But as the Apostles died monarchical local episcopacy — which had been introduced from the very beginning in some churches — became the general system. The bishop was the head of the church, the shepherd of the faithful, and, as successor of the Apostles, he had the fullness of the priesthood and the authority necessary for governing the community.

3. The key to the unity of the churches scattered throughout the world, which together made up one, universal Church, was the institution of the Roman primacy. Christ, the founder of the Church — as was pointed out elsewhere — chose the Apostle Peter as the firm rock on which to base his Church. But the primacy conferred by Christ on Peter was in no way a temporary, circumstantial affair, fated to disappear when Peter died. It was a permanent institution, an earnest of the permanence of the Church, something that would be valid for all times. Peter was the first bishop of Rome, and his successor in the see of Rome also succeeded to the prerogative of the primacy, which conferred on the Church the monarchical constitution which Jesus Christ wished it to have always. The Roman church was therefore — and for all times — the centre of unity of the universal Church.

4. The way in which this primacy is exercised has naturally been conditioned, over the centuries, by historical circumstances. In periods of persecution or when communication was difficult, the exercise of the primacy was less easy, less intense, than when times were better. But history allows us to document, from the very beginning, both the local churches' recognition of the pre-eminence of the Roman church and also the consciousness the bishops of Rome had of their primacy over the universal Church.

At the beginning of the second century, St Ignatius, bishop of Antioch, wrote that the Roman church was the church 'placed at the head of charity', thereby attributing to it a right of supremacy over the whole Church. For St Irenaeus of Lyons in his treatise *Against Heresies* (*c.* 185), the church of Rome enjoyed a singular pre-eminence and was the touchstone for judging what the true teaching of the faith was. In the first century we can find an outstanding indication of how aware bishops were of their primacy. In connection with a serious internal problem in the church of Corinth, Pope Clement I intervened with authority: his letter, laying down the procedure to be followed and requiring obedience of his instructions, is a clear proof of how aware he was of his primatial authority; no less significant is the respectful and docile acceptance given to the pope's intervention by the church of Corinth.

5. 'Christians are not born, they are made,' wrote Tertullian towards the end of the second century. These words may mean, among other things, that at that time the great majority of the faithful were not — as would be the case from the fourth century onwards — children of Christian parents, but rather people who had been Gentiles originally and had come to the Church by being converted to the faith of Jesus Christ. Baptism — the sacrament of incorporation into the Church — was at that time the last stage in a slow process of Christian initiation. This process, beginning with conversion, developed through a long 'catechumenate', a testing-time and a period of catechetical instruction, which was the established procedure from the end of the second century. The liturgical life of Christians centred on the eucharistic sacrifice, which was offered at least every Lord's day, whether in a Christian household — the seat of some 'domestic church' — or in places set aside for worship, which began to exist from the third century.

6. The early Christian communities were made up of all sorts of people, without any class or other kind of distinction. From Apostolic times, the Church was open to Jews and Gentiles, rich and poor, free men and slaves. Nevertheless it is true that most Christians were people of humble condition. Celsus, a pagan intellectual hostile to Christianity, mocked at the weavers, shoemakers, washermen and other uneducated types who were spreading the gospel in every sector of society. But it is an undoubted fact that even early on some members of the Roman aristocracy embraced Christianity: so much so, that one of Emperor Valerian's persecution edicts was specially directed against the senators, gentlemen and imperial officials who were Christians.

7. The internal structure of the Christian communities was hierarchical. The bishop — the head of the local church — was assisted by clergy, whose higher ranks — the order of priests and the order of deacons — were, like the episcopacy, of divine institution. Lesser clergy, who were assigned particular ecclesiastical functions, appeared in the course of the centuries. The faithful who made up the people of God were, in their immense majority, ordinary Christians, but there were distinctions among these also. In the Apostolic age, there were numerous charismatics — Christians who received exceptional gifts of the Holy Spirit with which to serve the Church. Charismatics played an important role in the primitive Church, but they were a passing phenomenon which practically disappeared in the first century of the Christian era. Throughout the period of the persecutions, the 'confessors of the faith' enjoyed special prestige: these were so-called because they had 'confessed' their faith as the martyrs had, but had survived imprisonment and torture. And there were Christian faithful whose life or ministries gave them a special status — the widows, who from Apostolic times formed an 'order' and looked after ministries to do with women; and the ascetics and virgins, who embraced celibacy 'for the love of the kingdom of heaven' and constituted, as St Cyprian put it, 'the most heavenly portion of Christ's flock.'

8. The first Christians suffered the severe external test of persecution; internally, the Church had to face no less a test — the defence of the truth against contemporary ideologies which sought to undermine the basic dogmas of the Christian faith. The early heresies — this was the name given to these currents of ideas — can be divided into three groups. There was an heretical Judaeo-Christianity, which denied the divinity of Jesus Christ and the redemptive effectiveness of his death: the messianic mission of Jesus, according to them, consisted in bringing Judaism to perfection by complete observance of the Mosaic law. A second group of heresies — which appeared later — was characterized by moral rigorism, fed by belief that the end of the world was at hand. In the second century, the best-known of these heresies was Montanism, although in Roman Africa at the beginning of the fourth century, extreme rigorism was also one of the features of Donatism.

9. But the greatest internal heresy the Church had to face during the age of the martyrs was, without doubt, Gnosticism. Gnosticism was a great ideological current tending towards that religous syncretism which was so fashionable during the last centuries of antiquity. Gnosticism — which was a real school of thought — claimed to be a higher wisdom accessible only to minority élites of initiates. Its policy towards Christianity was to distort the truths of faith by presenting gnostic teaching as the genuine expression of the most sublime Christian tradition — that teaching which Christ had given only to his most intimate diciples, those 'capable of understanding' what must remain hidden to the common run of faithful. The most notable exponent of Gnosticism was Marcion, who founded a pseudo-church which tried to imitate the Christian Church's structure and liturgy. The Church reacted energetically against gnostic infiltration of the Christian communities, while its theologians demonstrated the doctrinal incompatibility of Christianity and Gnosticism. By the end of the second century the Christians had definitively overcome the great temptation to let the faith be smothered by syncretic fantasies of the Gnosis. Christian faith had won its struggle against hellenistic wisdom.

5

Early Christian Writings

Christian literature began with the 'Apostolic Fathers,' whose writings reflect the way of life of the early Christians. The 'Apologists' wrote in defence of the faith and the third century saw the beginnings of theological writing in the strict sense.

1. The New Testament consists of twenty-seven books, all of them written in the second half of the first century. Four gospels cover the life and teachings of our Lord Jesus Christ; the Acts of the Apostles — written by St Luke — are also an historical record, dealing with the life of the early church of Jerusalem and going on to describe the activities of St Paul the Apostle up to his arrival at Rome to appear before the judgment seat of Caesar. A second group of books — didactic in character — consists of fourteen letters of St Paul and seven 'catholic' epistles — two by St Peter, three by John, one by James and one by Jude. A prophetic book — the Book of Revelation or the Apocalypse of St John — concludes the series of inspired books which contain the divine revelation of the New Testament. This inspired scripture is followed by early Christian literature.

2. Early Christian writing reflects the way of life of the early Church. As time went by, the growing Church had to face difficulties from within and without, and once it achieved a certain maturity it felt the need to develop a systematic exposition of the content of the faith. All this development occurred during the first three centuries of our era, before Emperor Constantine granted freedom of religion. The literary texts which have come down to us allow us to plot the various stages of this historical development.

3. The oldest of these writings came from a number of Greek writers, of the first and second centuries, known by the name of the 'Apostolic Fathers.' This title describes their special characteristics: their antiquity (some of these works were, probably, written before

St John's Gospel) and the close links between these writers and the Apostles (they may be considered disciples of the Apostles). The writings of the Apostolic Fathers are pastoral in character and are addressed to a Christian readership. The most outstanding texts in this first group of Christian writings are the *Didaché* (the oldest known account of church discipline), the letter of St Clement to the Corinthians, which we have already mentioned; the seven letters of St Ignatius of Antioch to other churches, written on his journey to Rome, where he would suffer martyrdom; and another letter, by St Polycarp of Smyrna. The *Shepherd* of Hermas, which has importance for tracing the history of penitential practice, also belongs to this group.

4. The early Church was the Church of the martyrs. The faithful were keen to have accounts of the heroism of those who had given their lives for the Christian faith. Undoubtedly their curiosity led to the concocting of legendary accounts, which have little value as history; but there are quite a number of documents about martyrs which carry every guarantee of being accurate. In many cases martyrdom was preceded by a judicial process in which notaries recorded magistrates' questions, the martyrs' replies and the sentence condemning them to death. Sometimes the Christians managed to obtain transcripts of these court documents: for example, this happened in the cases of St Justin, who was tried in Rome (*c.* 165), and of St Cyprian of Carthage (*c.* 258). Accounts of martyrdoms written by Christian eye-witnesses have the same sort of documentary value as these court *acta*; they consisted of a few touching pages which used to be read out in the churches on the anniversary of the martyr's death.

5. In the second century a new kind of literature grew up which shows the struggles of Christians against enemies from inside and outside the Church. The defence of the faith against heresy gave rise to a good number of anti-heretical writings. The most outstanding is St Irenaeus of Lyons' treatise *Against Heresies*, which we have already referred to and which is a refutation of gnostic teachings. Irenaeus placed key emphasis on the tradition conserved by the bishops, the successors of the Apostles, and especially the tradition of the Roman church, the teacher of the faith adorned with a special primacy over all the other churches.

6. The main objective of the 'Apologists' was to indicate Christian truth, and their writings were directed at readers outside the Church.

Some of these apologetic works, addressed to Jews, refuted Jewish
criticism of Christianity, arguing from the Old Testament to show
that Jesus was the messiah foretold by the prophets, that the Church
was the new Israel and that Christianity was the fullness of the law.
A notable example of this type is the *Dialogue with Trypho*, written
by St Justin Martyr around the year 150. But generally these writings
were addressed to the typical pagan hostile to Christianity.

7. The Apologists were a group of writers who took it upon
themselves to defend Christianity against the Gentile world. In
keeping with this purpose, they addressed themselves to people in
authority — emperors, magistrates — or to the Roman people in
general. The content of their writings was dictated by the kind of
accusations being levelled against Christians at any particular time.
To deal with accusations that Christians were guilty of all sorts of
crimes, the Apologists replied by giving an enactment of the real way
of life of Christ's disciples. The *Letter to Diognetus* (which may have
been the apologia presented by Quadratus to Emperor Hadrian)
presents this witness to the Christian way of life as the best proof
of the falsity of anti-Christian calumnies. Indeed, the author goes
on, the conduct of Christians is so admirable that the only explanation
can lie in the greatness of their ideals: 'they love all men, yet all men
persecute them; they are not known, yet they are condemned; they
are put to death, yet this gives them life; they are poor, yet they enrich
many; they lack everything, yet they have everything in abundance;
they are dishonoured, yet this very dishonour glorifies them.'

8. Christians were accused of being enemies of mankind and bad
citizens of the empire. The Apologists reacted vigorously against this
sort of attack: Christians, they wrote, bring a beneficial influence
to bear on society: 'what the soul is in the body, so are the Christians
in the world', was how the *Letter to Diognetus* argued, and Origen,
in his reply to Celsus, reaffirmed that 'the men of God [the
Christians] are the salt which binds together the societies of the
earth.' As far as the empire was concerned, the Apologists of the
second century claimed that the Christians were completely loyal:
they were exact in performing their duties as citizens and they offered
to emperors the very best they had to offer — their prayers: 'We pray
at all times for the emperors,' Tertullian wrote in his *Apologeticum*,
'that they may have long life, and we ask for benign government,
the security of the state, a strong army, a faithful senate, an honorable
people, peace in the world and whatever emperors and subjects may
desire.'

9. The Christians still faced opposition from intellectuals who saw little of intellectual value in Christianity. The Apologists' reply was that Christian teaching was a knowledge infinitely superior to Greek philosophy, for it held the complete truth. Around the year 200, some writers who had provided an intellectual defence of Christianity began to produce non-polemical literature, of a kind demanded by the growing maturity of the Church: expositions of the whole body of Christian teaching, to be used to educate the very many converts who began to come from more educated sectors of society. This was how the science of theology began.

10. If we had to assign a location to the origin of this science we would have to answer, unhesitatingly, Alexandria. In that cosmopolitan city, the focus of hellenistic culture, there grew up a famous theological school which, at the beginning of the third century, achieved extraordinary prestige under the leadership of Clement, a convert, whose great culture enabled him to expound the teaching of the faith within a structured, intellectual framework. The intellectual atmosphere of the Egyptian metropolis impressed its features on this Christian school — a preference for Platonic philosophy and the use of the allegorical method in biblical exegesis, in search of the deepest spiritual meaning of sacred scripture. All Alexandrian theologians have these characteristics.

11. Origen, the successor of Clement at Alexandria, brought this school to the peak of its prestige. Origen was an extraordinary person: a confessor of the faith, a most prolific writer, his intellectual reputation spread throughout the empire, to the extent that the mother of Emperor Alexander Severus sought to hear him lecture. He worked at an amazing pace, first in Alexandria and then in Caesarea in Palestine. Through St Jerome we know the names of eight hundred of the two thousand works he composed. His most ambitious undertaking, which took him his lifetime to complete, was the *Hexapla,* a sextuple version of sacred scripture aimed at establishing a critical edition of the Old Testament.

12. Quite distinct from the Alexandrian school was the school of Antioch, founded by Lucian of Somosata at the beginning of the fourth century. The theologians of Antioch rejected, in particular, the allegorical method so loved by the Alexandrians: they considered that it distorted the meaning of the biblical texts, running the risk of turning them into sheer mythology. The school of Antioch cultivated the literal meaning of scripture and found its inspiration in Aristotelian philosophy. These two schools — Alexandrian and Antiochene — were destined to impress their characteristic marks on the great theological questions to be posed the moment Christianity and the Church were able to live in freedom.

6

The Church in the Christian Roman Empire

In the course of the fourth century, Christianity began to be tolerated by the empire; then it formally obtained freedom; finally, in the reign of Theodosius I, it became the official religion. The Christian Roman emperor convoked great assemblies of bishops — the councils — and the Church was able to organize territorial structures for pastoral government.

1. Freedom came to Christianity and the Church when the echoes of the last persecution had hardly died away. Interestingly enough, it was Galerius, the main instigator of that last assault, who was the first to draw practical lessons from its failure. The successor to Diocletian as emperor, Galerius, when close to death, issued an edict from Sardica laying down new guidelines for state policy towards Christianity. This edict formally tolerated Christian practices: 'let Christians have the right to exist again,' it said, 'and to set up their places of worship, provided always that they do not offend against public order.'

2. The edict of Galerius, issued in 311, did not grant Christians full religious freedom. It simply tolerated them, in a cautious sort of way. Yet it was a very important milestone. For the first time Christianity ceased to be an 'unlawful superstition.' It had obtained citizenship. This was a victory of major significance; nothing like this had ever happened before. It is true that during the third century the Church had enjoyed periods of calm, and there had even been Roman emperors, like Philip the Arab (244-9) who were obviously well disposed to the Church; but at no time had the Church obtained any kind of formal recognition: she was always liable to new waves of persecution. This is why Galerius' edict was so important.

3. The transition from toleration to religious freedom happened very fast and was due mainly to Emperor Constantine. At the beginning of the year 313, Emperors Constantine and Licinius issued what has come to be known as the edict of Milan. This was not a legal statute in the proper sense; it was more of the nature of a political directive based on full respect for the religious choices of all subjects of the empire, including Christians. Legislation discriminating against Christians was removed from the statute book, and the Church, now recognized by the civil authorities, was able to recover places of worship and other property previously confiscated. Constantine thus became the man who inaugurated religious liberty in the ancient world.

4. Within this context of religious freedom. Constantine himself was moving gradually towards Christianity. Even before the edict of Milan, when the fate of the city and empire of Rome was in the balance with Constantine's army facing that of Maxentius, the former rode into the battle of the Milvian Bridge under the standard of the Christian cross. Constantine always considered his victory a sign from heaven, but he delayed his definitive conversion— i.e. reception of baptism — until many years later, just before his death (337). In the meantime his pro-Christian tendencies became more and more obvious. Immoral pagan practices or those involving the shedding of blood were declared illegal, and public magistrates were prohibited from taking part in traditional services of worship. Whereas the Church was given positive assistance in a number of ways — the building of churches, granting privileges to the clergy, help in re-establishing unity of faith (endangered by the Donatist schism in Africa and by Arianism in the east). The moral principles of the gospel began to provide the inspiration behind civil legislation: this marked the beginning of what is known as Christian-Roman law.

5. The advance of Christianity was not interrupted by Constantine's death — if one leaves aside Julian the Apostate's unsuccessful attempt to restore paganism. All the other later emperors — even those sympathizing with Arianism — were resolutely opposed to paganism. Gratian, shortly after he became emperor in 375, rejected the official title of *pontifex maximus* which his Christian predecessors had consented to retain. A particularly significant confrontation between ascendant Christianity and debilitated paganism occurred in the most venerable scenario of Rome — the senate. The altar of the goddess Victory, which presided over the chamber — a symbol of Gentile traditions — was removed on the decision of the Christian senators, now in a majority, despite opposition from their pagan colleagues. This religious evolution reached its final point before the close of the fourth century when Emperor Theodosius I promulgated an edict on 28 February 380 ordering all peoples of the empire to adopt catholic Christianity, now the only official religion of the empire. Whether it was good for the Church to be established in this way has been a subject of much debate, especially among commentators living in the pluralist environment of modern times.

6. Once it had obtained its freedom, the Church had to organize its territorial structures to cope with new pastoral demands: the world was now being Christianized rapidly. Applying what has been termed the 'principle of accommodation', the Church used the administrative structures of Roman cities as the basis of its own administration. Thus, the civil province became the model for the ecclesiastical province. By the fifth century the empire had more than 120 provinces. On this territorial framework the provincial division of the Church gradually emerged. The bishop of the capital of the civil province gradually acquired somewhat more weight than his colleagues in the other cities of the province. He was the metropolitan, the bishop of the metropolis, and the other bishops were his suffragans. In the sphere of law, the metropolitan was the court of appeal from other diocesan tribunals. And it was the metropolitan who ordained the new bishops of his province. It was also he who presided over the provincial council — the assembly of bishops of the region — which the first council of Nicaea laid down (though it was something not very well kept) had to meet twice a year.

7. The division of the empire into two parts — east and west — which occurred towards the end of the fourth century and which was later to lead to the formation of two separate empires, had deep effects on the life of the Church. The western part — which more or less coincided with regions Latin in culture and language — had only one Apostolic see, that of Rome. Consequently the bishop of Rome was also known as patriarch of the west. In the eastern part (Greek, Syrian and Coptic in culture) there were a number of great sees founded by Apostles (Alexandria, Antioch and Jerusalem) and these headed up patriarchates, that is, very extensive ecclesiastical jurisdictions. The first council of Constantinople raised the see of the city to the rank of patriarchate and attributed to its bishops a primacy of honour in the Church immediately after the bishop of Rome, the reason being, it said, 'that this city is the new Rome.' On this basis (non-ecclesiastical in character but, rather, political: the fact that it was the imperial capital) a new patriarchate was established which was destined to acquire undisputed pre-eminence among all the eastern patriarchates, especially after the council of Chalcedon.

8. Freedom allowed the Church to structure itself in a more organized way, and it also allowed the primacy of the popes over the whole Church to operate more effectively. The great popes of the fourth and fifth centuries — Damasus, Leo the Great, Gelasius — strove to specify exactly the dogmatic basis of the Roman primacy — the primacy granted by Christ to Peter, whose only legitimate successors were the popes. From the fourth century onwards, the Roman primacy was exercised very energetically over the churches of the west: the popes intervened time and again, through decretal letters or via legates and vicars. In the east, a great council (that of Sardica, 343-4) recognized the right of any bishop in the world to have recourse to the bishop of Rome as final court of appeal. But the general tendency was towards a strengthening of the jurisdictional autonomy of the patriarchates, especially that of Constantinople. The attitude of the Christian east towards Rome after the council of Chalcedon might be summed up in this way: attribution to the bishop of Rome of the primacy of honour in the whole Church; recognition of his authority in the area of doctrine; but a lack of awareness of any papal disciplinary or jurisdictional authority over the eastern churches.

9. Under the Christian Roman empire it was possible to hold great ecclesiastical assemblies (a genuine expression of the catholicity of the Church), which were given the name of ecumenical (world-wide) councils. Eight such synods took place between the fourth century and the ninth century, the first four of which are recognized as being particularly important — First Nicaea (325), Constantinople (381), Ephesus (431) and Chalcedon (451). All the councils were held in the Christian east, and most of the bishops who took part in them were from the east. Normally, the councils were convoked by the emperor, the only authority capable of providing the facilities needed for huge gatherings of this type; in some cases the emperor convoked the council at the pope's request and the papal legates occupied a position of honour in the council hall. Recognition of the ecumenical character of a great council was based on its reception by the Church as a whole as expressed particularly by papal confirmation of its canons and decrees.

10. The freedom of the Church and the conversion of the ancient world brought on to the scene a new factor which was to be particularly important in the future — the Christian emperor. Although he was simply a layman in the hierarchical order, the Christian emperor was keenly conscious of his role as defender of the Church and fosterer of Christian order in society — a role which Constantine attributed to himself when he assumed the title of 'bishop of the outside world'. The Christian emperors undoubtedly rendered great services to the Church, but they also interfered in ecclesiastical affairs to such extent that abuses occurred; extreme abuse of this type was termed 'caesaropapism.' These abuses were particularly serious in the churches of the east. In the west, the authority of the papacy, the weakness of western emperors and the distance between them and the east helped safeguard the independence of the Church. The relationships between the spiritual power and the temporal power, their harmonious cooperation, and the mission of the Christian emperor were discussed by many Fathers of the Church and especially by Pope Gelasius I in a letter to Emperor Anastasius. The Christian emperor's role as protector of the Church was regarded as so necessary during the centuries of transition from the ancient world to the middle ages that, when the emperors of the east ceased to provide the bishops of Rome with this protection, the popes looked to the kings of the French to take over this role.

7

The Christianization of Society

From the sociological point of view, the fourth century also witnessed profound religious change: the Christian communities of the earlier period gave way to a Christian society. In the Mediterranean world, Christianity ceased to be a religion of minorities; it became the religion of whole societies. Evangelization now extended out from the cities, reaching most of the rural populations. Very many rural churches grew up, giving rise to an ecclesiastical geography.

1. Freedom of religion, and the resulting conversion of the Roman empire to Christianity, had deep historico-social repercussions. At the start of the fourth century Christians were still only a small minority in the Roman world; although some regions were more densely Christian, it is likely that, overall, less than ten *per cent.* of the population was Christian. Under a pagan, persecuting empire, only people of real spiritual strength had the moral courage necessary to run the risk and accept the material disadvantages of conversion to Christianity. It was only from the time of Constantine onwards that crowds of ordinary, average people, found it easy to enter the Church.

2. Another aspect of the religious changes experienced in the course of the fourth century was a transition from the earlier system of religious communities to the phenomenon of a Christian society. Up to this, Christ's disciples had formed small communities in the middle of a pagan society. Now, over two generations, in the Mediterranean world which was the centre of the Roman empire, a process of Christianization of society took place. The step from a Church of small communities to a Christianized society might be seen — in terms of gospel similes — as the result of the silent, effective action of what was in its early stages a little yeast in a piece of dough, or a small mustard seed growing into a big tree. This phenomenon of the Christianization of society had enormous consequences.

3. The first of these was a new approach to the process by which people became members of the Church. In the preceding centuries the normal way people gained access to the Christian communities was by conversion after they had reached the age of discretion. Tertullian's remark that 'Christians are made, not born' would seem to suggest that in the late second and early third centuries the great majority of the faithful had been born pagans and had been 'made' Christians later. To cater for the admission of adults, the Church had created the catechumenate, a long period of ascetical and doctrinal training which prepared the neophyte for the reception of baptism, which was normally conferred at the great liturgical solemnities of Easter and Pentecost. The cathechumenate reached its high-water mark during the fourth century, when, from the reign of Constantine onwards, pagans flocked to the doors of the Church seeking baptism.

4. In the course of the fourth century it became quite common for people to be born into Christian families, and by the next century, in the whole Mediterranean world, this was the common pattern. This meant that the process of baptism changed considerably. Infant baptism became the general pattern — the children of Christian parents being baptized immediately after birth and therefore right through the year, without waiting for the big religious feasts to come round. The catechumenate went into rapid decline, since there were fewer and fewer ardent converts, and eventually it disappeared.

5. The spread of Christianity had started in the cities, the real centres of Roman life in classical times. This explains the urban character of most of the early Christian communities. When the Church obtained its freedom, the cities were rapidly Christianized and for a while there was a contrast between the population of the city — Christian — and that of the rural areas, which were still Gentile. It was at this time that the word *paganus* — a villager living out in the *pagus* — took on a religious meaning and was used — in opposition to Christian — to describe countryfolk who were still outside the Church, still holding on to their ancestral idolatrous traditions.

6. The Church's new-found freedom made it easier to propagate Christianity in rural areas and small towns. A great deal of missionary work was done, with St Martin of Tours (*c.* 316-97) as one of the outstanding missionary bishops. In catechizing these peoples, who were generally very uneducated, guidelines were followed which later proved useful for the conversion of the barbarian nations. The Church was careful not just to topple idols; it tried to ensure that no religious vacuums were left, and to do this it strove to Christianize people's deeply rooted social customs and traditional religious celebrations by finding a place for them within the sacramental discipline or in the annual liturgical cycle of the mystery of Christ and the solemnities in honour of the Blessed Virgin and the saints. Many Christian churches were erected on the sites of old pagan sanctuaries, that is, in those places to which from time immemorial the people of those areas had been going to worship their gods. Veneration of the martyrs and of the saints, and of relics (a tangible proof that these were men, not gods), which caught the imagination of these country people, also proved very helpful in the task of teaching Christian doctrine. Despite this, the evangelization of the rural population, subsequent to baptism, took a long time and much effort, so deep-rooted were the many superstitions and traces of idolatry intertwined with genuine religious sentiments.

7. In the first centuries of our era, the bishop had been the head of the local church, the pastor of a community rooted in a particular city. From the fourth century onwards, the bishop's function extended to rural populations also. This opened the way to the notion of diocese — a territorial area under the authority of a particular bishop — and thus an ecclesiastical geography came into being. The whole area of the Christianized territories was covered by this diocesan division, which meant that the limits of each diocese had to be specified. The notion of territorial competence developed, and church regulations urged bishops to exercise their jurisdiction within the confines of their dioceses and over only those persons residing in their dioceses, and not to interfere in the areas allocated to other bishops. The Christianization of the rural areas called for the construction of numerous churches and oratories, to attend to the spiritual needs of countryfolk. This led to the establishment of parishes and gave rise to the ordination of priests to look after the rural communities.

8. Another feature claiming our attention is the extraordinary importance the figure of the bishop obtained now that a Christian society had emerged. The people continued to see in the bishop a religious leader — but he also began to be regarded as their natural head and protector in all aspects of life. The crisis which occurred in the empire in the fifth century created an authority vacuum. In the dramatic final stages of antiquity, as civil administration broke down, the bishops perforce had to fill the breach, feeling obliged to intervene increasingly in social and political life. They had a particular responsibility to protect socially disadvantaged people, who were unable to defend themselves. As far as access to the episcopacy was concerned, the new order of things made it increasingly difficult for bishops to be elected 'by the clergy and people', as had been the normal thing when the bishop was the pastor of a small urban community. Now, although the old formulas continued to be used in the canonical documents, the appointment of bishops in practice fell to the diocesan clergy and the other bishops in each province, with emperors and princes frequently taking a hand. People prominent by virtue of their position in society or their family background often held episcopal sees in the Christian-Roman period and helped to enhance the social prestige of the episcopacy. A well-known example of this is St Ambrose who moved from being governor of upper Italy to being bishop of Milan; St Paulinus of Nola was a consul in his youth; Sidonius Apollinaris, the overlord of southern Gaul and son-in-law of Emperor Avitus, became bishop of Clermont.

8

The Dogmatic Formulation of Christian Faith

In the centuries following the conversion of the ancient world, precise definition was given to Christian teaching on basic truths of faith — on the Blessed Trinity, on the mysteries of Christ and on the question of grace.

1. The Christian-Roman period was extremely important from the point of view of doctrine. Now that the Church was free, the historic moment came for it to give precise formulation to orthodox teaching on basic questions of Christian faith — the Blessed Trinity, the mystery of Christ, and the question of grace. The definition of catholic dogma occurred in the context of heated theological battles against heresies which led to schisms in the Church, some of which are still with us.

2. The fourth century saw the formulation of dogma concerning the Trinity, with catholic orthodoxy having to confront Arianism. Arianism can be traced back to certain early doctrines which over-emphasized the oneness of God, to the extent of obliterating the distinction of persons in the Blessed Trinity (Sabellianism) or of 'subordinating' the Son to the Father, making him inferior to the Father (subordinationism). A radical subordinationism inspired the teaching of Arius, an Alexandrian priest (*c.* 250-336), who not only held that the Son was inferior to the Father, but went as far as denying that Jesus was God. The absolute oneness of God which Arius proclaimed led him to see the Word as simply the noblest of all created beings, not as the natural Son of God: Christ was God's adopted son and therefore only in an improper sense could he be called God.

3. Arian teaching was clearly influenced by Greek philosophy with its notion of the Supreme God — *Summus Deus* — and a concept of the Word very akin to Plato's demiurge, a being intermediate between God and the universe who was the shaper of creation. This connexion between Arianism and Greek philosophy accounts for its rapid spread and for its being welcomed by rationalist intellectuals involved with hellenism. Arianism had very serious consequences on Christian teaching, affecting as it did the dogma of the redemption: for if the incarnate Word, Jesus Christ, were not God, then redemption would be ineffective. The church of Alexandria realised the seriousness of the problem and, after attempting to dissuade Arius of his error, it proceeded to condemn him at a synod of the bishops of Egypt (318). But Arianism was already a world-wide problem and it led to the convoking of the first ecumenical council in history.

4. The first council of Nicaea (325) was a clear victory for the defenders of orthodoxy, two of the most outstanding of whom were bishops — Ossius of Cordova (Spain) and a deacon (and later bishop) of Alexandria, Athanasius. The council defined the divinity of the Word, using an unambiguous term to describe his relationship with the Father — *homoousios*, 'consubstantial.' The Nicene symbol or creed proclaimed that the Son, Jesus Christ, 'God from God, Light from Light, true God from true God, begotten, not made,' is 'consubstantial' with the Father. Orthodoxy's victory at Nicaea was followed, however, by a post-council period of a radically opposed viewpoint, which constituted one of the most surprising episodes in Christian history. The pro-Arian party, led by Eusebius, bishop of Nicomedia, managed to exert a decisive influence at the imperial court and in the last years of Constantine's reign and during the reigns of his successors it looked as if Arianism was going to prevail. The most outstanding of the Nicene bishops were exiled and, as St Jerome graphically put it, 'the whole world groaned and discovered to its surprise that it had become Arian.'

5. From the middle of the fourth century on, Arianism was divided into three factions: the radical Anomoeans, who laid emphasis on the dissimilarity of the Son with respect to the Father; the Homoeans, who regarded the Son as *homios* — that is, 'like to' — the Father; and what are called semi-Arians — those nearest orthodoxy — for whom the Son was 'substantially like' the Father. The theological work of what are called the Cappadocian Fathers developed the teaching of Nicaea and attracted many supporters of the more moderate tendencies in Arianism, with the result that in a very short time Arianism disappeared from the horizon of the universal Church, surviving only as the form of Christianity professed by most of the Germanic nations who had invaded the empire. The theology of the Trinity was completed at the first council of Constantinople with the definition of the divinity of the Holy Spirit (in reaction to another heresy — Macedonianism). Thus, by the end of the fourth century, catholic doctrine on the Blessed Trinity had been fixed in the form of Niceno-Constantinopolitan creed. However, there was one aspect of Trinitarian theology not expressly dealt with in the Creed — the relationships between the Holy Spirit and the Son. This would later give rise to the famous *Filioque* problem, which was to become an apple of discord between the Christian east and the Christian west.

6. Once the doctrine of the Blessed Trinity had been defined, theology had to deal with the mystery of Christ, not in relation to the other divine persons, but in regard to the nature of Christ himself. The basic problem was this: Christ is perfect God and perfect man; but how do divinity and humanity combine in man? On this question, the two great theological schools of the east took opposite sides. The Alexandrian school laid emphasis on the perfect divinity of Jesus Christ: his divine nature so penetrates his human nature — like fire heating an iron — that an internal unity results, a kind of 'mixture' of natures. The Antiochene school stressed, instead, the perfect humanity of Christ: the unity of the two natures in him is only external or moral in such a way that rather than speak of 'incarnation' it would be more correct to speak of the 'indwelling' of the Word, who 'dwells' in the man Jesus as inside a garment or a tent.

7. This Christological problem came out in the open when Nestorius, the bishop of Constantinople, who belonged to the Antiochene school, preached in public against the divine maternity of Mary, refusing to give her the title of *Theotokos*, 'God-bearer,' Mother of God; she was, he said, only the *Christotokos*, 'Mother of Christ.' This led to popular demonstrations and the denunciation of Nestorius' doctrine to Rome by St Cyril, the patriarch of Alexandria. Pope Celestine I asked Nestorius to retract, which he refused to do. The council of Ephesus (431), now summoned by the emperor, Theodosius II, had a very rough passage due to rivalry between Alexandrine and Antiochene bishops; but eventually agreement was reached and a profession of faith was composed for which was formulated the doctrine of the 'hypostatic union' of the two natures in Christ and Mary was acknowledged as Mother of God. Nestorius was deposed and sent into exile; however, groups of his followers continued to exist in the near east forming a Nestorian church which carried out a great deal of missionary work, over a number of centuries, in countries of Asia.

8. By the first half of the fifth century the patriarchate of Alexandria had grown in power and many of its bishops took an active part in the internal affairs of the church of Constantinople itself. It also happened that after the death of St Cyril extremist tendencies gained the upper hand in Alexandria. The Alexandrian theologians were unhappy about the Ephesus teaching on the two natures in the one person of Christ, due to their understanding two natures as being equivalent to two persons: they claimed that there was only one nature in Christ, because in the incarnation the human nature had been absorbed in the divine. When this doctrine — monophysitism — was preached in Constantinople by the archimandrite Eutyches, Flavian the patriarch deprived Eutyches of his office. The patriarch of Alexandria, Dioscorus, then intervened, with the support of Emperor Theodosius II. An unruly council was held at Ephesus (449) under the presidency of Dioscorus; the patriarch of Constantinople was deposed and exiled; a dogmatic letter sent to Flavian by the pope, by the hand of two papal legates, was prevented from being read, and the doctrine of the two natures in Christ was condemned. The pope, Leo the Great, gave this council a name which was passed into history — the 'latrocinium of Ephesus.'

9. As soon as Emperors Pulcheria and Marcian succeeded Theodosius II, Pope Leo asked that a new ecumenical council meet: this was the council of Chalcedon (451). This council adhered unanimously to the Christological teaching contained in Leo the Great's letter to Flavian: 'Peter has spoken through the mouth of Leo', the fathers proclaimed. Chalcedon's profession of faith recognized that there were two natures in Christ 'without their being any confusion or division or separation between them.' But monophysitism, far from disappearing, put down deep roots in various parts of the east, especially in Egypt, where it was used as a secessionist banner against the authority of the empire. The condemnation of monophysitism was taken as an attack on the traditions of Athanasius and Cyril. A monophysite patriarchate grew up in Alexandria (supported by the monks and the indigenous Coptic population) in opposition to the melchite or imperial patriarchate.

10. This historical context explains why the succeeding emperors strove to find compromise formulas which, without contradicting the symbol of Chalcedon, would be more acceptable to the monophysites and would thereby assure the loyalty of the population of these areas to the empire. Examples of this were the *Henotikon* — an edict of Emperor Zeno (482) — and the famous question of the 'Three Chapters', proposed unsuccessfully by Justinian, which produced unfavourable reactions in the west. The most serious effort in this direction was that backed by Emperor Heraclius, an energetic defender of the Christian east against the Persians and Arabs. Sergius, patriarch of Constantinople, thought that, without denying Chalcedonian teaching on the two natures, it could be held that, by virtue of the hypostatic union, there was in Christ only one divine-human activity (monoenergism) and that Christ had only one will (monothelitism). Heraclius sanctioned this doctrine by his dogmatic decree *Ecthesis* (638). But *Ecthesis* solved nothing, neither in the field of religion nor in that of politics. The monophysites rejected it, and in a very short time Palestine, Syria and Egypt were in the hands of the Arabs. The Christological debate came to an end when the third council of Constantinople (the sixth ecumenical council), on the basis of letters sent by Pope Agatho, completed the symbol of Chalcedon with an express profession of faith in the two activities and two wills of Christ. Monophysite Christianity still lives on in Egypt and Ethiopia.

11. These Trinitarian and Christological controversies took place mainly in the east. The only major theological question posed in the west was that of grace — centering on the relationships between divine grace and human freedom, and therefore on the parts corresponding to God and to man in personal eternal salvation. Pelagianism — which took its name from Pelagius, a monk — tended to minimize the role of grace and over-optimistically exalted human nature's capacity for good: human nature was not damaged by original sin; that sin was the personal sin of Adam and had not been transmitted to his descendants. The great adversary of Pelagianism was St Augustine, who in combating it made a decisive contribution to the foundation of catholic teaching on grace. But St Augustine (in the flush of the polemic), in his effort to stress that the grace of salvation was a free gift of God, went as far as saying that God's salvific will was not general to all but particular to individuals and that the elect obtain salvation not through their personal merits being taken into account but through the irresistible efficacy of grace. These propositions of Augustine are in no way offical church teaching. The catholic teaching on this subject was formulated by the second council of Orange (529) and confirmed by Pope Boniface II. The council declared that man by his own efforts alone is incapable of effecting supernatural good; but it rejected the doctrine of God's particular salvific will and it explicitly condemned so-called 'predestination to evil.'

9

The Fathers of the Church

*The fourth and fifth centuries were the golden age of patristic writing.
In east and west a whole series of remarkable men emerged, noted for
holiness of life and outstanding work in the area of the sacred sciences
and even of culture in general.*

1. History always has its protagonists and the ecclesiastic history
of the Christian-Roman period had outstanding ones. The enormous
effort involved in formulating dogma, as described in the last chapter,
resulted from the wisdom and work of a series of exceptional
personalities, who are described as 'Fathers of the Church.' The
Fathers combined sacred science with personal holiness publicly
recognized by the Church. This differentiates them from plain
'ecclesiastical writers', whose holiness or complete orthodoxy is not
guaranteed. The golden age of patristic writing was the fourth and
fifth century, although the term 'the age of the Fathers' extends to
the seventh century. The western Fathers wrote in Latin; most of
the eastern Fathers wrote in Greek, although others used Syrian,
Coptic, Armenian, Georgian, Arabic etc. In this chapter we will refer
only to the Greek and Latin Fathers whose reputations spread
throughout the universal Church.

2. The Greek patristic period opens with a writer who must be
considered the founder of the science of Church history — Eusebius,
bishop of Caesarea in Palestine (+ 339). Eusebius of Caesarea has
been immortalized by his book *Ecclesiastical History*, a treasure-trove
of information about the first three centuries of Christian history.
A younger contemporary of Eusebius, St Athanasius (+ 373) was
the main champion of the Nicene profession of faith. He devoted
his life to the defence of orthodoxy against Arianism: as far as his
writings are concerned, his three *Discourses against the Arians* deserve
special mention, but the best proof of Athanasius' dedication is the
five periods of exile he underwent for his fidelity to catholic orthodoxy.

3. On the theological plane, victory over Arianism was won mainly by the work of three Fathers who, like Athanasius, belonged to the neo-Alexandrian school, and who are called the Great Cappadocian Fathers. They are Basil of Caesarea (330-79) and his brother Gregory of Nyssa (335-94) and their friend Gregory of Nazianzus (+ 389/390). Basil was outstanding not for his writings alone but also as an administrator and as an organizer of monastic life in the east; Gregory of Nazianzus, the 'Christian Demosthenes', is famous for five theological discourses in defence of the divinity of the Son and of the Holy Spirit. Gregory of Nyssa, the most profound theologian of the three, was one of the fathers of Christian mysticism.

4. Born and trained in Antioch, St John Chrysostom (344-407) is regarded by the Greek Church as its outstanding preacher and as an eminent exegete who produced commentaries on many books of the Bible. Bishop of Constantinople for six years, his homilies earned him the enmity of Empress Eudoxia and he was deposed and died in exile. The most famous Egyptian Father of the fifth century was undoubtedly St Cyril, bishop of Alexandria (412-44). Cyril upheld orthodox teaching against Nestorius and, for his defence of Mary's title of Mother of God, he must be regarded as the main mariologist among the Fathers of the Church.

5. The first of the great Fathers of the west, a man of exceptional historical importance, St Ambrose (*c.* 339-97), produced much interesting biblical exegesis and was famous for his preaching, but he was also a man at the centre of public affairs during a time of political upheaval. Ambrose was a true Roman: this can be sensed both in his brilliant career and in his pastoral government of the see of Milan, to which he was raised by popular acclaim, when still a catechumen. St Ambrose had the exceptional honour of conferring baptism on one who would become the most outstanding of the Latin Fathers, St Augustine.

It was also his fortune to be friend and adviser to three emperors and to excommunicate one of them, Theodosius the Great, for his massacre at Thessalonica; but at Theodosius' funeral he spoke a moving eulogy, as impressive as his one for Valentinian II, the previous emperor. Ambrose's fame spread far beyond Milan and increased the prestige of that see not only in northern Italy but in other parts of the Latin west.

6. The Roman west also produced the greatest student of sacred scripture: Eusebius Jerome (342-420), a Dalmatian. It should be pointed out that Jerome, like most of the Fathers of the Church, did not live a secluded life of recollection, concentrating on study and uninvolved with what was happening around him. He lived for periods in Antioch, Constantinople, Trier and Rome, and eventually settled in Bethlehem, the birthplace of Jesus. Nor was Jerome only a researcher and scholar. He was a passionate polemicist and, through spiritual direction, energetically promoted asceticism among the women of the Roman aristocracy. Jerome is famous as a historian and exegete, but his greatest legacy was the translation of many books of the bible direct from Hebrew or Aramaic into Latin. This version is known as the Vulgate: its authenticity, declared by the council of Trent, means that in matters of faith and morals it is free from error.

7. But the outstanding Father of the Church and one of the really prominent figures in Christian history and indeed in world history, was Aurelius Augustine (354-430), from North Africa. His *Confessions* — a spiritual autobiography from childhood up to his conversion — is a masterpiece of world literature, which has kept its modernity century through century. St Augustine wrote commentaries on the Old and New Testaments and made significant contributions in all the main areas of theology. A man of his time, Augustine questioned himself about the events taking place before his very eyes, particularly the collapse of the Roman empire in the west, laid waste by barbarian invasions just when it was becoming a Christian empire. Pagans interpreted these misfortunes as a punishment from the gods for abandoning the old religion. In reply, Augustine wrote *The City of God*, an essay on the theology of history and a treatise on apologetics in which he tried to discuss the meaning of history and the plan of divine providence. In his old age St Augustine personally experienced the severity of his time and died in his episcopal city of Hippo when it was being besieged by the Vandals.

8. The Fathers of the western Church also include two popes whom history describes as 'Great': Leo and Gregory. Leo I, as we have seen, played an important part in the formulation of Christological dogma. To him also is attributed much of the theology of the Roman primacy and its scriptural basis in the primacy conferred by Christ on Peter. The other 'great' pope, Gregory (540-604), was a Roman already on the threshold of the middle ages. In a few centuries the world had changed a great deal: if the historical context of the first Father of the Church, Athanasius, was the Constantinian empire, the horizon of Gregory the Great was not so much distant Constantinople as Lombard Italy, Visigoth Spain and Merovingian France. Gregory's works — the *Book of Morals* and the *Dialogues* — were avidly read in the middle ages; and 'Gregorian' chant lasted in the Church up to our own time. A Spaniard — St Isidore of Seville (+ 636) — can be considered the last western Father. His *Etymologiae* constituted the first Christian encyclopaedia and his mission can be seen as that of teacher of the medieval west, to which he introduced the riches of the wisdom of the ancient world.

10

Christianity and the Barbarian Nations

Invasions by Germanic tribes gave Christianity access to new peoples who established themselves in territories previously controlled by the empire. Later missionaries brought the gospel beyond the limits of the old empire. Germans, Slavs, Magyars and others received the Christian faith and entered the Church, although some of them did so through first professing Arianism.

1. The barbarian invasions were a very important event in Christian history. Up to this point, the spread of the gospel had virtually been limited to peoples of Mediterranean culture, with a few rare exceptions, such as Armenia. From the close of the fifth century, the huge eastward migrations of peoples which occurred had the virtue of putting the Church into contact with a new cultural and ethnic world. Germans and Slavs, Magyars and Scandinavians espoused Christianity in the course of the following centuries. The invasions opened up whole new horizons for the spread of Christianity. A contemporary — Paul Orosius, a disciple of St Augustine — described how providential these upheavals were, which others saw only as a tragedy: 'Even if the barbarians had been sent into Roman territory,' he wrote, 'with the sole design of filling the Christian churches of east and west with Huns, Suevi, Vandals and Burgundians and countless other multitudes of Christian believers, we would have to praise and exalt the mercy of God for having brought to the knowledge of the truth (though at the cost of our ruin) so many nations which, if they had not come to it by this route, would surely never have reached it.

2. Most of the German tribes which invaded the west were not directly converted to Christianity from their ancestral paganism: they passed through an intermediate stage of Arian Christianity. The background to this important page in European religious history was that Arianism found its way into the German world via the Visigoths.

In the year 376, this people, who were located in Dacia and were being hard pressed by the Huns, sought permission of Emperor Valens to cross the Danube (the frontier of the empire at that time) and establish themselves on imperial territory. According to the historian Jordanis, the Visigoths offered to recognize Valens' authority and to live peaceably with the Romans; better still, they said, they were ready to become Christians if he sent them missionaries who spoke their language.

3. Valens allowed the Visigoths to settle in Thrace and Moesia; and, since he was an Arian, he sent them missionaries from his own sect. The Gothic-Arian community, led by their bishop Ulfilas, were very influential. Ulfilas invented the Gothic alphabet and translated the bible into that language, which up to then had not been a written language. Provided with this excellent tool for catechesis, the missionaries from the school of Ulfilas spread their teaching among the Visigoths, with the result that by the end of the fourth century they had been completely Arianized. This was precisely the time when Arianism as a theological problem was disappearing from the scene in the Church as a whole. Paradoxically this fact help Arianism take root among the Germans; it became their national religion — one more factor differentiating the minority German invaders, who had the political upperhand, from the majority indigenous population, who were Roman and catholic. Arianism thus became the religion of almost all the Germanic peoples settled in the lands of the western empire. Some of these — Vandals and Ostrogoths — remained Arians until they were extinguished in the sixth century. Others had enough time to finish their spiritual itinerary, through a second conversion to Catholicism. This was the case with the Suevi of Galicia and with the Burgundians, in the sixth century, and the Visigoths in the time of Recared (589). Arianism persisted among the Italian Lombards until far into the seventh century.

4. In this historical context we should notice the importance of the conversion of the Franks. At the same time as all the Germanic kingdoms of the west were embracing Arianism a young and vigorous people burst on to the religio-political scene in the person of the Franks. These were pagans who, in the second half of the fifth century, spread over the north of Gaul where through their victory over Burgundians and Visigoths they established what was to be the kingdom of Franks, France. But they opted for Catholicism, not Arianism. At Christmas around the year 500, Clovis, the king of the Franks, received catholic baptism. This event had tremendous repercussions among the indigenous population of these old Roman territories: '*fides vestra, nostra victoria est* (your faith is our victory),' Avitus, bishop of Vienne, wrote exultantly to Clovis. Avitus, who enjoyed great prestige and was a member of the senatorial aristocracy of Gaul, had made a very acute observation; for the conversion of Clovis had very important subsequent effects: from now on, no longer would there be only one catholic monarch in the world, the emperor in the east; the west would have its own — the king of the Franks.

5. In some places the barbarian invasions pushed back Christianity — for example, in Roman Britian, which was overrun in the fifth century by the Anglo-Saxons, who were pagans and whose conversion was undertaken much later, on the initiative of Pope Gregory the Great. But the same fifth century saw the evangelization of Ireland and this injected new life into the Christianity of Celts elsewhere. This time also marked the spread of the gospel beyond the frontiers of the old empire of the west into territories which had never been ruled by Rome and among the peoples that occupied them. In the seventh century the initiative came from Irish and Scottish missionaries, with St Columbanus the most outstanding figure. In the eighth century, Anglo-Saxon missionaries took over from the Celts and spread Christianity in those parts of Germany which were still pagan. An English monk, Winfrid — who changed his name to Boniface — was the great apostle of Germany, whose patron he still is.

6. Christianity continued to spread in the centuries that followed, reaching peoples in central and eastern Europe. Normally — as was the case with Clovis and the Franks — the conversion of a nation coincided with the baptism of its leader, whose example very many would follow. Thus, the conversion of the Magyars came about with that of their king, St Stephen; that of the Bohemians with St Wenceslaus; and of the Poles with their leader, Mieszko. However, the Christianization, properly speaking, of such peoples was a lengthy process, helped by the conversion of the leader, but really taking centuries. Both the Latin Church and the Church of Byzantium strove to evangelize the Slav nations — sometimes clashing, as was the case with the Bulgars; but there were some truly admirable figures, such as the brothers Cyril and Methodius, whose apostolic work was solemnly confirmed by papal authority. By and large, it can be said that the western Slavs adhered to the Latin Church, while the eastern Slavs, evanglized by Byzantine missionaries, stayed within the ambit of the patriarchate of Constantinople. The main Christian conquest of the Greek Church was that of Russia, and the baptism of Grand

Duke Vladimir (972-1015) can be taken as the point when the people of Russia were converted.

7. The Christianization of Scandinavia and the Baltic countries marks the last chapter in the conversion of Europe. Early missionary endeavour in the ninth century by the French Emperor Louis the Pious was frustrated by the Vikings, or Norsemen, who harassed the coasts of the west. Viking paganism was not of the traditional kind; it took the form of a vigorous and virulent attack on Christianity, with the hammer of Thor as the counter-standard of the cross. The Vikings who settled in the British Isles or in French Normandy were the first to be Christianized. And these produced a native clergy which proved the best way to begin the evangelization of their country of origin. However, significant pagan outposts survived in Sweden until the twelfth century and in eastern Prussia and the Baltic countries until perhaps the fourteenth century.

8. The Mediterranean countries suffered a very different religious onslaught in the seventh century — the Islamic invasion. Islam, founded by Muhammad (570-632), spread with amazing speed after his death. The Muhammadans overpowerd most of the Christian east, dominated north Africa from Suez to the Atlantic, and then overwhelmed Visigoth Spain. Poitiers in central France, where they were defeated by Charles Martel, marks the furthest point of their penetration into western Europe. But, although Europe north of the Pyrenees managed to stem the tide, the Moorish presence in the Iberian peninsula lasted nearly eight centuries and both the near east and northern Africa still form part of the Islamic world. For the most part the spread of Islam occurred in Christian countries. The Muhammadans did not forcibly convert Christians, because they regarded them, as they did the Jews, as peoples of 'The Book', that is, the Bible, a book sacred to all three religions; but the tolerance which they offered Christians was cautious and grudging: this was the experience of the Spanish Mozarabs. The various churches coped unequally with the test of Islamic domination, which became more severe as hopes of a Christian restoration receded and more and more people conformed to Islam. The churches of the east — especially the Coptic or monophysite church which was deeply rooted among the indigenous population of Egypt — has managed to survive to the present day. But the saddest story is that of Christianity in Latin Africa — that of St Cyprian and St Augustine — which faded out after an agony which lasted centuries.

11

The Ascetical Life and Monasticism

From the very beginning of Christianity there were Christians who embraced a life of complete imitation of Jesus Christ. Later, Christian asceticism adopted forms associated with abandonment of the world and with life in community: this was how monasticism started. The monastic life flourished from the fourth century onwards, in both east and west.

1. Christian ascetical life is coextensive with the Church of Jesus Christ. From the very beginning, some Christians, of both sexes, embraced a way of life aiming at exact imitation of Jesus Christ: they kept virginity or continence, practised prayer and Christian mortification and engaged in works of mercy. In the first three centuries, ascetics and virgins did not live in common; they stayed in the world. Without any public ceremonies, such as were later introduced, they committed themselves to keep chaste 'for the sake of the kingdom of heaven' (Mt 19:12) and lived among the other members of the Christian community, in their own homes, owning property and earning their living by work.

2 In the Christian-Roman society of the fourth and fifth centuries asceticism flourished even in the ranks of the aristocracy. Married couples of senatorial nobility, like Paulinus of Nola and Therasia or Pinian and Melania divested themselves of vast inheritances and sought to conduct themselves as faithful disciples of Jesus Christ in keeping with the teachings of the gospel. St Jerome was spiritual director to various groups of Roman noblewomen, first in Rome and later in Palestine: he took them through sacred scripture and encouraged them in the practice of Christian asceticism. The cultivation of chastity by women increased throughout the fourth century, with widows and young maidens sometimes living common life (in Rome, for example, Paula and Marcella were the focus of this development).

3. From the early fourth century, this Christian ascetical tradition led to the institution of monasticism, which was to play such an important part in the history of the Church. This new form of ascetical life had one special characteristic — abandonment of the world. Perfect consecration to God's service, it was now thought, could only occur through distancing oneself from the world. Now that the Church enjoyed external peace, the general level of spiritual life was lower than that of earlier Christian communities, due to the influx of large numbers of neophytes who were on the mediocre side and somewhat pagan in their habits.

4. Egypt used to be regarded as the cradle of monasticism but recent research suggests that monasticism was an indigenous phenomenon in a number of different regions. However, there is no doubt that Egypt had great influence on the development of monasticism everywhere. There, as elsewhere, anchorities retired into the desert, famous spiritual teachers gathered disciples around them, and colonies of solitaries (called 'lauras') grew up with a church building in the centre. Athanasius' *Life of Anthony*, which spread all over the east, is both a biography and an apology for monasticism which did much to extend the fame of Coptic monasticism all over the Christian world.

5. In Thebaïd — Upper Egypt — St Pachomius (286-346) gave monasticism two additional features of enormous importance in the history of asceticism — common life and obedience to a religious superior. Pachomian monks founded numerous monastic communites in which, contrary to the kind of independence typical of the solitaries, the monks' lives were minutely ordered by written regulations —the 'rule' — which was to become an essential element in monasticism. The Rule of St Pachomius was reformed in a stricter sense by Abbot Shenoute. In Asia Minor, where monasticism had made its appearance shortly after it did in Egypt, St Basil of Caesarea was its promoter and organizer. Basil did not write a rule as such, but his ascetical lectures and other writings constituted sets of monastic regulations which were also called rules; these acted as the main basis of Byzantine monasticism and had an influence also in the west.

6. In the Latin west, monasticism, among men and women, flourished from the fourth century onwards. A famous nun, Etheria (author of the *Itinerarium*, a detailed account of her journeys through the east) was an intrepid pilgrim, who probably came from Galicia. Monasticism sprang up in out-of-the-way places, such as those at Ligugé and Marmoutier in Gaul, founded by St Martin of Tours, and often these became centres of rural development. The search for solitude led monks to establish monasteries on offshore islands, like the famous Lérins, near Cannes, or Cabrera in the Balearic islands or the foundations on Scelig off the Irish coast or Iona in Scotland. In contrast to these coenobites who settled in out-of-the-way places, there were others whose monasteries were located within city walls or in the suburbs, where the cloister acted as the wall of separation ensuring the solitude which was an essential part of monastic profession. Some eighty monasteries could be counted in Constantinople in the time of Justinian, among them the famous Studion, whose monks (called Studites) were very influential in the church life of Byzantium. In the west, the foundations of John Cassian, author of two famous books, the *Conferences* and the *Institutes* were located in the city of Marseilles. From Visigoth Spain a homily on 'perfect monks' survives, which is an apologia for city-based monasticism.

7. Many famous bishops, such as St Ambrose of Milan and Eusebius of Vercelli, fostered monastic life among the clergy of their churches. An outstanding example of this was St Augustine who, after becoming bishop of Hippo, brought his clergy together in his home and established a system of life in common. The so-called Rule of St Augustine, devised for this community, was taken as a standard rule in medieval centuries when various attempts were made, by way of reform, to encourage community life — *vita canonica* — among the clergy. The attitude of monks towards culture varied: whereas in Egypt the tone was anti-intellectual, there were monasteries, such as that at Vivarium, founded in Calabria by Cassidorus (a former minister of Theodoric the Great) where study played a main role — anticipating the contribution which medieval monks made to the conservation of earlier culture.

8. In the history of western monasticism the place of honour must go to St Benedict (480-547), the father of western monasticism. First at Subiaco and later at Monte Cassino, monasteries were founded and governed by St Benedict. In Monte Cassino, towards the end of his life, he devised the famous rule which bears his name, which was based on a combination of his own experience and elements taken from the great eastern founders — Pachomius and Basil — and on an anonymous text, the *Rule of the Master*; this rule constitutes the main source of the Benedictine code. This code, over the years, was outstandingly successful and became the typical rule of western monasticism.

9. The Benedictine tradition became so widespread in medieval Christianity that it supplanted even the memory of other ancient western traditions. Two of these traditions deserve special mention on account of the considerable influence they had in the history of the Church — Celtic monasticism and Visigoth monasticism. The Irish church, after the death of St Patrick, adopted a marked monastic structure, adapted to the nature of the tribal society which obtained in Ireland at the time. The Rule of St Columbanus was the main Celtic monastic code and missionary monks carried it with them into the heart of continental Europe. In Spain, St Martin of Braga, in the second half of the sixth century, brought to Galicia the teachings of eastern monasticism. In the catholic Visigoth kingdom, Spanish Fathers composed various rules — such as that of St Leander for virgins, dedicated to his sister Florentina; that of St Isidore for the Honorian monastery in Baetica; that of St Fructuosus of Braga, and what is known as the 'common' rule also associated with his influence. Fructuosus was the most famous of all the Visigoth monks and he gave the impetus to an ascetical movement which survived the Islamic invasion. Pactualism, congregations of monasteries and a trend towards joint monasticism (for men and women) are the characteristic features of Spanish monastic tradition.

12

Christianity in Feudal Europe

Christianity suffered the imprint of feudalism in the troubled times that marked the first stage of the middle ages. Churches and the holders of benefices became implicated in the close network of relationships which provided the structure of feudal society. Interference by secular nobles in ecclesiastical life produced a moral decadence which led, in Rome, to what has been called the 'Iron Age' of the papacy.

1. The eighth century witnessed a profound change in the history of western Christianity, caused primarily by new relationships established between the Holy See and the Frankish kingdom. The eastern empire, which still had important dominions in Italy, had for centuries been the secular protector of the papacy and of its territories — the so-called 'patrimony of St Peter', — which had always been under threat from restless neighbours, in the form of the Lombards. But this protection became more and more ineffective as the empire, growing every more easternised and worn out by constant pressure from Islam, paid less and less attention to the west. In need of a new 'secular arm', the papacy turned its eyes towards the only western kingdom — after the collapse of Visigoth Spain — capable of performing this function: the kingdom of the Franks, whose leader Avitus of Vienne foresaw, after the baptism of Clovis, as being the catholic monarch of the west.

2. Circumstances were just right for this development. Pepin the Short, the powerful *major domus* of the French court, in the year 750 approached Pope Zachary on a matter of doctrine fraught with political implications: who, he asked, was the more worthy to be called king: he who was king only in name [the last of the Merovingians] or he who effectively held power [that is to say, Pepin himself]? The pope's reply brought the reign of the Merovingians to an end and marked the birth of Carolingian France. In 753, Pope Stephen II gave kingly anointment to Pepin and his two sons, Carloman and

Charles, the latter two receiving the title of 'Patrician of the Romans' which gave them the power to play a part in the government of Rome and to watch over the states of the Church, the territory covered by the temporal power of the popes.

3. The process begun in this way peaked during the reign of Pepin's son, Charlemange, one of the great shapers of medieval Christianity. On Christmas day 800, Charles was crowned emperor in St Peter's by Pope Leo III. The coronation of Charles was an event of immense significance: after a lapse of three centuries the western empire was born again, facing the Greek empire of the *basileus* of Constantinople. The new empire, whose capital was at Aachen, was Latin-Germanic but above all it was a Christian empire, with the emperor having, as his principal mission, the protection of the Church and the Roman see.

4. Charlemange's empire suffered from a congenital weakness due precisely to its being the brain-child of such a remarkable personality. Very soon after his death it began to decay due to territorial distributions, a weakening of central authority and a crisis in society: imperial order gave way to feudal disintegration, for which the Church also paid the price. As sovereign authority evaporated, the dangers of anarchy increased and threats from Norsemen, Saracens and Magyars multiplied. The ordinary people, unable to defend themselves, sought protection from the only source available, the class of armed nobility which had monopolized real, effective power. A tightly knit system of vassaldom grew up, with patronage exacting the price of service, creating the structure of feudal society.

5. Ecclesiastical structures also suffered the impact of feudalism. The nobles sought to nominate rectors and to benefit financially from their 'own churches' which they had built in their domains for the religious service of the rural population; and they also tried to exercise similar rights over other churches and monasteries to which they gave patronage and protection. The larger magnates wanted to have control of ecclesiastical revenues to use them to reward their soldiers, or to be able to appoint relatives and favourites as holders of bishoprics and abbeys, positions much sought after by the nobility because of the social influence they involved. These repeated abuses were not anti-Christian in intention; those responsible for them were sincere, if uneducated, Christians; but they did lead to a noticeable secularization of ecclesiastical life and a general moral impoverishment.

6. The most typical example of the impact of feudalism on the Church and on Christian society was the so-called 'Iron Age' of the papacy. This lasted from the beginning of the tenth century to the middle of the eleventh, with a temporary improvement in the second half of the tenth century. The eclipse of imperial authority left the Roman see without a protector and allowed it to fall victim to the dominant feudal factions in Rome. Powerful noble families — the family of Theophylact, the Crescentii, the Tusculani — exercised a tyrannical oppression over the papal see, in an attempt to control it in the same manner as the feudal lords controlled their 'own churches.' The 'patrician' Theophylact, the 'senators' Theodora and Marozia, the 'prince of all Romans' Alberic, disposed of the pontificate as their whims took them: even adolescents and people of utter incompetence and unsuitability occupied the papal chair. The fact that the papacy survived this test and even in its worst moments did not deviate on doctrine of faith and morals must be seen as a clear indication of divine assistance to the Church.

7. But all was not disorder and darkness in these difficult times of the genesis of feudalism which are also known as the Dark Ages. A number of historical developments were in fact germinating at this time which would combine to produce the religious and cultural splendour of medieval Christendom. One of these factors was the foundation of a monastery destined to have enormous influence over the social and spiritual life of the west — Cluny. Monastic renewal in the Carolingian era, fostered by a Visigoth, Benedict of Aniane, had sunk without trace in the violence of the feudal abuses, when the secularization of the monasteries made it impossible for genuine religious life to survive. Cluny was founded in 909 by Duke William of Aquitaine; it depended directly on the pope, being 'exempt' from any lesser authority, ecclesiastical or lay. Cluny was very successful and many other monasteries submitted to the authority of this abbey or were founded from it. The so-called 'Order of Cluny' spread all over the west until it counted over 1,200 monasteries and a whole army of monks, so much so that the order has been described as a 'monastic empire'. The Cluniac monks — the 'black monks' — were an essential factor in the movement of Christian renewal which began towards the end of the eleventh century.

8. Another development destined to have a deep influence on the history of European Christianity had begun in Germany, also at the beginning of the tenth century. When the last traces of the Carolingian past had disappeared, the German dukes, in 919, re-established the kingship, choosing Henry I, duke of Saxony, as king; his son, Otto I (936-73), a great monarch, must, likē his predecesor Charlemagne a century and a half before, be considered one of the great builders of Christian Europe. Otto waged successful military campaigns against Slavs and Magyars, who became his vassals, and established his authority in the heartland of his kingdom. As a climax to his career he was crowned emperor in Rome, in February 962, and thus a German empire succeeded the Carolingian as the Christian empire of the west. Otto I assumed the mission of protecting the papal states and he also took control of elections to the papacy, thereby protecting them from interference from the Roman nobles. This situation obtained also during the reigns of Otto II (973-83) and Otto III (983-1002); and although the premature death of the latter allowed the Roman factions to interfere once again, the rights of the emperor were claimed forty years later by the energetic Henry III, allowing him to bring to an end once and for all feudal control of the papal see.

13

The Slow Gestation of the Eastern Schism

The division of the Roman empire brought into the open the ever-latent dualism between west and east, the Latin world and the Greek, Rome and Constantinople. This dualism was also reflected in the ecclesiastical and religious sphere where tensions provoked an increasing separation, eventually leading to confrontation and schism.

1. In the seventh century, as a consequence of the spread of Islam, three of the four eastern patriarchates fell into the power of the Muhammadan empire — Alexandria, Antioch and Jerusalem. The loss of Egypt and Syria meant that the monophysite and Nestorian confessions were further distanced from contact with the universal Church. These communities, situated in lands which formed part of the Islamic world, now lived an almost completely separate existence. Therefore, the Christian east from this time forward became synonomous with the Byzantine or Greek Church, that is to say, the patriarchate of Constantinople and the churches which derived from its monastery activity, which recognized in it a primacy of jurisdiction or at least of honour. It is this eastern, Greek Church whose relations with Rome up to the schism of Cerularius we shall now discuss.

2. The classical Roman empire was able to envisage the world as a united whole, based on the countries and peoples of the Mediterranean area. But underneath this unity there lay profound differences between the cultures of the Latin west and the hellenic east. In the interests of more effective government, Diocletian's administrative reform at the end of the third century officially recogized two parts to the empire, one eastern, one western, coincidental with these two cultural areas. This division, to which we have already referred elsewhere, ended up in the creation of two empires, whose historical destinies would later prove so different from one another.

3. Christianity also suffered the effect of this counterposition of east and west, of Greek culture and Latin culture. At the basis of these divergences we can notice the marked contrast between the pragmatic temperament of the Latins and the speculative turn of mind of the Greeks. Another disturbing factor exacerbated this dialectic — a growing failure in communications due to language difficulties. For the first three centuries of Christianity Greek had been the language of the Church; but from the end of the third century — and beginning in Carthaginian Africa — Latin was introduced into the literature and language of the Church, and in the fourth century all western liturgy was conducted in Latin. The lack of a common language not only created a spiritual distance between Christian east and west but also gave rise to an atmosphere of suspicion and resentment between the two, in a period fraught with heresy and theological controversy. Differences in discipline and in rites, very obvious to the people, also contributed to accentuate this dualism and mutual distrust.

4. But the main factors responsible for tension — and for discord — between Christian east and Christian west was the exaltation of the patriarchate of Constantinople. The famous canon 28 of the council of Chalcedon (which was not accepted by Pope Leo the Great) gave the see of Constantinople authority and jurisdiction over all the territories of the Byzantine empire not dependent on the other three eastern patriarchates, on the grounds that Constantinople was the 'New Rome', capital of the empire and residence of the emperor. Thus, Constantinople became the principal patriarchate of the the Christian east, emulator of the Roman papacy, closely bound to the empire of Byzantium, while Rome became more and more separated from that empire and looked to French or German emperors for protection. In this context of increasing coldness between the two churches, frictions and confrontations marked the stages of a long process of weakening of ecclesiastical communion.

5. A first break in relations between Rome and Constantinople came in the fifth century — the schism of Acacius, which was motivated by the Monophysite proclivities of that patriarch (482) and lasted thirty years. The repercussions of the iconoclastic controversy were more prolonged. As is known, Leo III the Syrian – a great emperor who saved Byzantium from the Arab threat — caused a grave religious crisis which affected the life of the Christian east for more than a century. In 726 he prohibited the veneration of sacred images and soon afterwards ordered their destruction. Byzantine Christendom was torn into two irreconcilable groups, the iconodulists and the iconoclasts, venerators and destroyers of images. Leo II tried to get the pope to sanction the iconoclastic edicts and when he received an unambigious refusal he took reprisals against the Roman church. However, the battles over images had not unfavourable results on relationships between eastern Christians and Rome: the defenders of images — who included the monks and the great mass of people — looked to the papacy for support, and their most distinguished defenders — St Theodore the Studite and the patriarch Nicephorus — and the second council of Nicaea itself (787) — the seventh ecumenical council — recognized the primordial role of the pope as teacher of faith to the whole Church. But understanding between Rome and Constantinople was decidedly not helped by the Bulgar question.

6. The Bulgar question arose in the context of rivalry over the see of Constantinople between two patriarchs, Ignatius and Photius. The prince of the Bulgars, Boris, was converted to Christianity in the year 864 and he sought the despatch of missionaries to work to convert his people. Boris turned first to Constantinople, and then he changed his mind and offered, to Pope Nicholas I, to incorporate his people into the Latin Church, under the jurisdiction of Rome. A later misunderstanding led the rather fickle Boris to dismiss the Latin missionaries and turn once more — this time definitively — to union with the patriarchate of Constantinople, whom Bulgaria would later follow at the time of the schism. Naturally enough these events further strained relations between Rome and Constantinople.

7. Although they were marginal to the Bulgar question the confrontation between the patriarchs Ignatius and Photius contributed to the disimprovement of Rome-Constantinople relations. Ignatius and Photius succeeded each other twice in the see of Constantinople, following swings in eastern politics. Pope Nicholas I's support of the legitimate rights of Ignatius provoked a violent reaction on Photius' part — a veritable declaration of war against the Latin Church. In recent years Catholic studies of Photius have vindicated his orthodoxy. However, even admitting that the relationships of the Byzantine Church with the papacy were not formally broken during Photius's second patriarchate, it is not possible to exonerate him from responsibility for distancing the Christian east from Rome. Photius, knowing that it would drive a deep wedge between Greeks and Latins, chose as his weapon the question of the *Filioque*, condemned its inclusion in the Creed used by western Christendom and accused the west of heresy. The result was that no longer would differences between Greeks and Latins be limited to matters of discipline and liturgy: they would also cover matters of dogma, with the net result that the unity of the Church was permanently compromised. It is right to say that Photius, an eminent savant who personified the true ecclesiastical spirit of Constantinople, contributed more than anyone else to preparing the minds of people for the future eastern schism.

8. The split eventually came about, not very dramatically, at the beginning of the Gregorian era. The pronounced anti-Latin outlook of the patriarch of Constantinople Michael Cerularius and the failure to understand the Byzantine mentality on the part of the papal legates (Humbert of Silva Candida and Frederick of Lorraine), sent to negotiate ecclesiastical peace, were the immediate causes of the break. On 16 July 1054, Humbert placed a bull of excommunication on the altar of the church of Santa Sophia; eight days later Cerularius and his patriarchal synod replied by excommunicating the legates and those who had sent them. The schism was now out in the open, although it may well be that many people at the time — and perhaps even the protagonists themselves — thought that this was just one more in the long series of previous instances of troubled relationships between Rome and Constantinople. Certainly, for the great mass of Christians, both Greek and Latin, the start of the eastern schism passed quite unnoticed.

9. As time went by, Christians discovered that a genuine schism had taken place, breaking the ecclesiastical communion between the Roman papacy and the Greek Church. From that time forward the restoration of unity was a permanent objective of Christendom. It was fostered by popes, desired in Constantinople by emperors and men of the Church; councils met to negotiate union; and there were moments — the second council of Lyons (1274) and the council of Florence (1439) when it seemed as though the long-sought union had been attained. It never really happened, but it was not until Constantinople fell to the Turks and the empire of Byzantium disappeared (1453) that the desire — and hope of — terminating the eastern schism and rebuilding Christian unity came to an end.

14

Papacy and Empire in the Middle Ages

The papacy and the empire were the two pillars on which medieval Christendom rested. The pope represented spiritual authority, and the emperor, temporal authority. The ideal — seldom fully attained — was understanding and harmonious cooperation between these two authorities.

1. In medieval Europe, Christendom meant all the peoples united by the bond of the faith, forming a broad spiritual and cultural community, over and above differentiating characteristics and divisions into nations and kingdoms. Political theory during this epoch regarded Christendom as a living organism, at whose head were two supreme authorities — the pope, the holder of spiritual power, and the emperor, the holder of temporal power. The mission of both was that of general government of the Christian peoples and of helping men — each authority in its own sphere — to attain their last end.

2. A deep sense of unity existed among the peoples who made up Christendom, until the lower middle ages, when nation states and sovereigns made their appearance. However, Christendom never really became a supranational institution, and the kings of France and England never regarded themselves as subject to the emperor, though they did form part of western Christendom. And in the Spain of the reconquest the title of emperor borne by Alfonso VI and Alfonso VII was a clear statement of independence, an indication that they recognized no higher power on earth. Moreover, even in the very centre of the Christendom system relationships between the two supreme authorities were never easy and sometimes they came into open conflict with each other.

3. In theory the relationship between papacy and empire is easy to understand: the German king, designated by the prince electors, was crowned emperor by the pope; the emperor, in turn, ensured that papal elections were properly conducted. And pope and emperor, each in his own sphere, wielded the supreme authority appropriate to him. Discord arose from the fact that, historically, each tried to obtain the absolute primacy in Christendom. The Iron Age, as we have seen, brought the papacy to its lowest point, from which it was rescued by imperial intervention. The energetic Henry III played the leading role in Christendom when he changed the system by arrogating to himself as 'patrician of the Romans' the faculty of nominating the pope. The canonical election of the nominee and popular acclamation of him became only formalities, to keep in line with tradition. Suidger of Bamberg (Clement II) and his immediate successors were all nominated in this way. Henry always chose German bishops for the papacy; but his nominations were good ones and these German bishops restored both dignity and prestige to the office and prepared the way for the Gregorian reform.

4. However, the papacy (once restored) could not be happy with this imperial primacy in Christendom, or accept as a definitive solution this sort of dependence on the emperor. The German popes and Roman ecclesiastics who set about the renewal of the Church — under the leadership of St Peter Damian and the monk Hildebrand — constituted a reform party, with 'the freedom of the Church' as its catch-cry. The premature death of Henry III (1056) made it possible for the head of the ecclesiastical body (the papacy) to regain its freedom and for papal elections to escape from imperial control. But this liberation had still to be extended to the whole body of the Church — and this, effectively, was the programme of the Gregorian popes and especially of Hildebrand, who became pope as Gregory VII.

5. In the view of Gregorian reformers the clergy was suffering from three abuses — nicolaitism (non-observance of the law of clerical celibacy); simony (buying and selling spiritual ministries); and lay investiture. The last-mentioned consisted in the disposal of ecclesiastical offices by lay people who held title from secular authority — emperors, kings, lords, owners or patrons of churches. This abuse the Gregorian reformers saw as being the cause and root of the other evils; which was why they considered it necessary to put an end to investiture and the consequent appointment by lay people of holders of spiritual offices. Such was the origin of the 'investiture controversy', which brought confrontation between papacy and empire and, in particular, between Pope Gregory VII and Emperor Henry IV.

6. Investiture, as we shall see, was a very complex problem. It seemed to be totally inadmissible (certainly this was the Greogorian view) for a lay person to be able to confer an ecclesiastical office along with which went a degree of spiritual authority. Moreover, in practice, investiture implied that the layman selected the person to hold the office, and this inevitably lowered the moral level of the clergy. But it was not quite as simple as that, when looked at from the emperor's point of view. Otto I, in an effort to stabilise his German kingdom (always at risk from the dukes, who often felt they would prefer independence), had conferred public offices and seigneurial rights on the great German ecclesiastics — so that now, along with a spiritual ministry, they were also temporal princes. The inevitable authority attaching to the offices of bishop and abbot in Germany explains why the monarchs were so interested in reserving to themselves the investiture of higher ecclesiastical offices, since they played such an important part in the life of the empire. The investiture struggle extended beyond the life-times of its protagonists, Gregory VII and Henry IV; a solution, the *pactum Calixtinum*, was reached by the concordat of Worms (1122) arranged by Pope Callistus II and Emperor Henry V. It was agreed that the provision of bishops should be by way of canonical elections. The person elected would receive ecclesiastical investiture from the metropolitan bishop (through handing over ring and crozier, the signs of his spiritual power); whereas lay investiture was reserved to the monarch (this was symbolized on his handing over the sceptre, as the sign of regalian rights). Time was to show that this solution was not good for ecclesiastical life, since it meant that episcopal appointments were controlled by the German nobility who had a dominant influence in the chapters which constituted electoral colleges.

7. The investiture problem was one of the main arenas of the Gregorian struggle to free the Church; but its solution was only a first step in a much bigger plan of Gregory VII to establish 'Christian justice' in the world, thereby allowing the kingdom of God to be fully realized on earth. As the pope saw it, the direction of this enterprise was the responsibility of the papacy, on the grounds of the basic Gregorian axiom that supremacy in the world belonged to the papacy, the bearer of spiritual power in Christendom, and that this supremacy — the 'fullness of power' — also covered the whole sphere of things temporal. The theses of this Gregorian doctrine are summed up in the twenty-seven propositions of Gregory VII which are given the name of *Dictatus papae*. (At that time, there was a general acceptance of the genuineness of the *Donation of Constantine*, a forged document which purported to transfer temporal sovereignty over the west to the pope: this strengthened Gregorian claims to papal supremacy.)

8. The papacy and the empire were the two supreme institutions in the politico-doctrinal system of Christendom. As we have already said, the harmony between them essential for achieving their common good was seldom obtained: more often than not they were in dispute over whose rights took precedence. The thick volumes of *Libelli de lite* in the *Monumenta Germaniae Historica* indicate the amount written on both sides during this polemic. But, in addition to this, we must remember that relationships between popes and emperors did not affect the whole of Christendom: normally the scenario was the empire, that is, the German countries and a large part of the Italian peninsula. In lower Italy were to be found the states of the Church, which were a guarantee of the freedom of the Apostolic See and its main source of revenue. Popes and emperors, therefore, were not only dealing with doctrinal questions about who came first; they also had to work out a way of maintaining political peace with each other in the context of a confined geographical area. These specifically Italian problems soured relations between papacy and empire and played their part in the disintegration of Christendom. In the twelfth century, the struggle between Pope Alexander III and Emperor Frederick Barbarossa smacked of confrontation between Italy and Germany, with the great cities of northern Italy, who formed the Lombard League, taking the side of the pope. In the thirteenth century, the reintegration of lower Italy (Naples and Sicily) into the empire caused the papacy grave anxiety; the popes felt the Hohenstaufen emperors were too close for comfort, bordering as they did the papal states to both north and south. The result was confrontation between the popes and Frederick II — with tragic consequences for the empire, and also for the papacy. This conflict played a key role in breaking down the system of medieval Christendom.

15

The Zenith of Christendom

The Gregorian reform prepared the way for the zenith of Christendom — the twelfth and thirteenth centuries, bestriding the pontificate of Innocent III. Christian Europe was at its most vital: ecumenical councils met, universities were founded, as were great religious orders, and Christian kings and princes joined together in the crusades.

1. The twelfth and thirteenth centuries are the classic age of medieval Christendom. Bestriding the two centuries, one single figure best symbolizes the sense of achievement that marks the period — Innocent III (1198-1216). The supremacy of the spiritual power, envisaged by the Gregorian doctrine, became a reality at the time of this pope, with kings and peoples submitting to his authority. Innocent III exercized this authority with a firm hand and he had no compunction about resorting — with success — to spiritual weapons when princes strayed from the path of justice: he put France under interdict, to force King Philip Augustus into matrimonial fidelity; he managed to force the submission of John Lackland, the English king; and England, like Aragon and Portugal, declared themselves vassals of the Holy See; in Germany, Innocent arbitrated on which of two candidates should be given the throne; in Naples and Sicily he acted as guardian of the future Frederick II. Innocent III's authority was exercised over all Christendom and was received everywhere with respect and obedience.

2. If there were one single characteristic which epitomises the classic age of medieval Christendom, it must be, undoubtedly, its amazing vitality. It is as if a great wind was blowing through the Church and through Christian society, renewing its human and spiritual strength and imbuing it with a wonderful spirit of creativity: as if powerful energies, which had lain dormant for centuries, burst open the doors and brought an immensely fruitful new spring to the western world. We will take a look at some of the more significant events that occurred during this explosion of new life, because these events, more than any hyperbole, show us what this great age of Christendom was like.

3. The era of European Christendom was a time of councils. None of the councils of the first millenium had taken place in the west; whereas six ecumenical councils were held during this new period: four Lateran councils, two at Lyons; and even a seventh — at Vienne (1311-12) — though it occurred in the fourteenth century, must be included in this conciliar century. Unlike the earlier councils, these were all convoked and presided over by the pope, and they dealt with matters of discipline concerning the life of the clergy and of the faithful in general — rather than with doctrinal questions. The fourth council of the Lateran, called by Innocent III in 1215 and attended by more than 400 bishops and an even larger number of abbots and capitulars, along with representatives of the Christian princes, was the outstanding assembly of medieval Christendom, meeting at the moment that marked the zenith of that society.

4. One of the signs of the spiritual vitality of the period was the great blossoming of religious life. The Cluniac monks had acted as a germ of ecclesiastical renewal in the tenth century, and in the next century they were the great monastic resource used by the papacy of the Gregorian reform. Also in the eleventh century, St Bruno founded Chartreuse (1084), which he conceived by a kind of synthesis of the solitary and the coenobitic life. And the great creation of the twelfth century was the Cistercians, a new branch of Benedictinism aspiring at a return to primitive simplicity. Alongside Cluny, which kept all its splendour, with its Romanesque churches and majestic liturgy, the white monks of Cîteaux cultivated the land and built abbeys in an early Gothic style reflecting the simplicity of their spirit. Cîteaux was given a great boost when a young Burgundian aristocrat, Bernard, took monastic profession there and soon was appointed abbot of Clairvaux. St Bernard was probably the most important European personality of the twelfth century, exercizing an immense influence over the life of the Church and of Christendom. The Cistercians, who had hardly a dozen abbeys when Bernard joined them, had 343 by the time he died, and the community of Clairvaux alone had almost 700 monks.

5. If the eleventh and twelfth centuries were the time of the monasteries, the thirteenth was the century of the friars. It is significant that at the very moment that Christendom seemed to have reached maturity, when the papacy had attained its maximum degree of temporal power and the profit motive was inspiring the new bourgeoisie, at precisely that moment men like Francis and Dominic emerged to re-establish evangelical poverty as the basic virtue of the religious life. The mendicants did not work the land like the Cistercians: they renounced ownership of any kind and sought to live on the charity of the faithful. The mendicants were not monks but friars, and they made their appearance just when a new economic and social climate was taking shape in the west. It is symptomatic that the founder of the Cistercians, Bernard, was a Burgundian noble, whereas a century later Francis was the son of a cloth merchant of the city of Assisi. The mendicants did not found monasteries away out in the peace of the country: their convents were right inside the cities and they dedicated themselves, by preference, to pastoral work in the now populous cities which had obtained a new lease of life. St Francis (+ 1226) founded the order of 'Friars Minor', which was approved by Innocent III in 1209; the other great mendicant order, the order of 'Preachers', founded by St Dominic Guzman and approved by Honorius III (1216) had, as its original vocation, the defence of the faith, and the Dominicians gave special importance to theological studies. Christendom was enriched still further by other mendicant orders, such as the Carmelites, the Augustinians or those dedicated especially to the ransoming of Christians captured by Muhammadans.

6. The centuries of Christendom were also the classical age of theology and canon law. Scholastic theology — the science of the 'school' — was born towards the end of the eleventh century with the aim of forging a new vision of the world based on reason and divine revelation; it had its own, 'scholastic', method, in the form of a dialectical argument concluding in a synthesis. The great names of early scholasticism are those of St Anselm, Peter Abelard, and Peter Lombard. But the golden age of scholasticism was the thirteenth century, and its great achievement the construction of Christian Aristotelianism. This undertaking, initiated really by St Albert the Great (*c.* 1200-80), was accomplished by St Thomas Aquinas (1226-74), the key figure in theology (alongside St Augustine), whose writings fixed the foundations of a catholic view of the world and of life which is still basically valid today.

St Thomas' masterpiece was the *Summa Theologiae*, which displaced all the other medieval *Summae*. In his encyclical letter *Aeterni Patris* (1879) Pope Leo XIII declared that St Thomas stands out above all other doctors, whose work he brought to completion and reduced to a single unified whole; for this reason, the pope laid down that the doctrine of the Holy Doctor should be used as a basis for courses in centres of ecclesiastical studies. Later popes and the second Vatican council have repeated these doctrines. St Bonaventure (1217-74) and Duns Scotus represent a Franciscan school of theology (contemporary with Thomas Aquinas), Platonic-Augustinian in inspiration. In the field of canon law, Gratian, around the year 1140, finished his *Decretum*, a systematization of traditional law. New law was codified by St Raymond of Penafort in the *Decretales* of Gregory IX (1234). These and other later collections made up the *Corpus juris canonici*, a compilation of church law used right up to the proclamation in 1917 of the first Code of Canon Law.

7. Medieval Christianity not only fostered the development of the sacred sciences but also created the institution whose specific aim is to develope and spread advanced knowledge and culture — the university. Corporations of traders and students, established as *studia generalia*, were given public recognition by civil and ecclesiastical authority. The University of Paris was the first to go through this process and in 1215 Innocent III confirmed the privileges which guaranteed its authority. Oxford, Bologna, Salamanca and other universities acquired this status in the course of the thirteenth century. Universities had a pronounced supranational character, which reflected the universalist spirit of Christendom: their teachers came from different countries as did the students, who formed groups of 'nations', according to their background.

8. The most characteristic undertaking of Christendom was the crusade. Usually, crusades were not the initiative of any particular kingdom but rather a common effort of the whole of Christendom, under the direction of the pope. who conferred special graces on those taking part. The spectacle of princes and peoples setting out for the east, eager to liberate the Holy Sepulchre, is an impressive proof of the deep religious spirit of the middle ages. The crusades ended in failure; but the mere fact that certain motivations, among which Christian idealism prevailed, could give rise to such a remarkable phenomenon is itself enough to justify the crusades. In the Iberian peninsula the popes also granted crusade privileges to the soldiers of the reconquest; but this cannot be regarded as a supranational enterprise, although outsiders did join these Iberian crusades at certain times. It is interesting to note that the end of the crusades coincided with the beginning of missions in Islamic lands. Armed struggle against the infidel gave way to peaceful proclamation of the gospel in these missions, which were the initiative of the mendicant orders.

16

Structures of a Christian Society

Christianity influenced every level of medieval society. The warrior was transformed into the knight, and military orders arose from among the knights. Artisans formed unions and brotherhoods, which later became guilds. The Christian people built cathedrals and went on pilgrimage to Jerusalem, Rome and Compostela.

1. It would not be correct to conceive the centuries of medieval Christendom as a golden age in the sense of being so inspired by the ideals of the gospel that it was an almost perfect expression of the kingdom of God on earth. The reality was quite different: these times were full of personal sin and wretchedness, full of disorders and injustices. But it would be even further from the truth to ignore the extent to which Christianity imbued the lives of the people of the time and their social and family structures. After the age of barbarism which followed the invasions and the collapse of the ancient world, after the centuries of anarchy which saw the genesis of feudalism, feudal society itself was a genuine if imperfect Christian society, representing immense progress both in the religious and in the cultural order.

2. Medieval Christendom put a high value on peace, and fostered peace in society. In the centuries of barbarism, a climate of violence dominated social life and legal relationships: self-reliance and family vengeance were accepted as normal and even consecrated by written law, and private wars were chronic and interminable. But then a concerted effort was made to install peace in social life: the Truce of God forbade every form of violence on certain days and periods of the year; the Peace of God protected persons and places of asylum. This movement for peace, initiated by the Church, was seconded during the latter half of the eleventh century by the princes, who backed up with civil punishments the spiritual sanctions which were already being applied. In a society like that of the middle ages, in which the warrior class had a monopoly of strength and power, Christianity strove to harness this power in the cause of peace and good. The warrior caste constituted an 'order' of society — the Christian knightly class. The warrior turned knight was to be the natural protector of the weaker members of society and the champion of all just causes.

3. The religious idealism of the knightly class found its most developed expression in the military orders, another creation of European Christendom. These orders were born of a union between monastic profession and the office of bearing arms that belonged to the medieval nobility. The powerful military orders were the Templars and the Hospitallers. Both of these began in Jerusalem and both played an important part in the crusades. St Bernard was an enthusiastic promoter of the Templars, dedicating to them a moving eulogy entitled *De laude novae militiae*. The power and wealth which the Templars later amassed was the cause of their ruin: King Philip the Fair organized the celebrated trial of the Templars with the aim of appropriating to himself the wealth they owned in France, and he obtained from the Avignon Pope Clement V the dissolution of the order (1312). The Hospitallers survived the crusades and were important in the struggle against the Turks in the Mediterranean. The island of Malta later gave its name to this body of knights, because it was their headquarters until its occupation by Napoleon at the end of the eighteenth century. Other military orders did not have this supranational character — the Teutonic knights, who were established in eastern Prussia from the thirteenth century; and the various orders which arose in Iberia during the reconquest.

4. The resurgence of city life led to the growth of a city population made up of free men of modest social condition, particularly craftsmen and small merchants. These formed associations, strongly religious in inspiration, with charitable purposes and as self-help organisations; and Christian influence among the people in general led to countless brotherhoods and confraternities which also sprang up in the world of work. Guilds had well-defined purposes to do with the regulation of work but their members were also bound by ties of brotherhood and by religious welfare obligations similar to those existing among members of confraternities. Guilds bonding together people of the same trade, under the patronage of a saint, strengthened Christian influence in the core of these work relationships.

5. Forms of piety which have endured into our own time were shaped in the centuries of Christendom: foremost was attendance at mass on Sundays and days of obligation, already a religious duty going back a considerable time; the fourth Lateran council (1215), now fixed the obligation of yearly confession and communion. There were quite a lot of fast days and days of abstinence. The general faithful paid tithes on their crops, for the financial support of the Church. Eucharistic piety and veneration of the Blessed Virgin and other saints were prominent features of the spirituality of the time. In the thirteenth century Corpus Christi was established as a major church festival; in the eleventh century the hymn *Salve Regina* was composed, and later the Rosary emerged and became a widespread practice. The feastdays of saints, including local saints, were widely celebrated, and pious literature achieved immense success.

6. The pilgrimage was another characteristic expression of medieval religious spirit. Christians felt attracted to visit the holy places, despite the inevitable discomfort and danger involved. The Holy Sepulchre in Jerusalem, the tombs of the Apostles Peter and Paul in Rome and the tomb of St James the Apostle in Santiago de Compostela were the main places of pilgrimage. These pilgrimages always contained a strong penitential element; people went on them to atone for their sins and gain merit in God's eyes. The penitential efficacy of the pilgrimage increased when, in 1300, Boniface VIII decreed a jubilee to mark the new century: all pilgrims to Rome could gain a plenary indulgence — an extraordinary grace previously reserved to those who went on crusade or helped the crusade in some way.

7. Religion also influenced medieval art. In fact it can be said that, with a few exceptions, the art of the middle ages was Christian and religious. Europe built huge cathedrals in episcopal cities and sometimes quite impressive churches in towns and villages. The plastic arts — painting, sculpture, stained glass, mosaic — acted as a major form of catechesis which put the truths of dogma and of salvation history within reach of the people, whether educated or uneducated.

17

Heresy in the Middle Ages

Heresy can be found even in the heart of western Christian society. Religious currents, eastern in origin, became very influential in the south of France; the Inquisition was created to combat them and to defend the unity of the faith. Other heterodox doctrines which spread in the lower middle ages may be regarded as precursors of Protestantism.

1. Unity of faith was a dominant characteristic of the religious life of the west during the first centuries of the middle ages. Once Germanic Arianism had died out and other peoples had been converted from their ancestral paganism, only individuals or very small groups were the exception to the catholic Christian unanimity of Europe. Although it may seem paradoxical, it was not until the high point of Christendom — from the twelfth century on — that heresy, as a social phenomenon, appeared once more on the scene.

2. Some of these heretical shoots were connected with the great movement towards Christian poverty which affected the Church in the twelfth and thirteenth centuries. One result of this movement was the mendicant orders and the spread of the Franciscan spirit among people of all walks of life. But Franciscanism also had its extreme expressions which gave rise to radical groups — Humiliati, Fraticelli — closely linked with the Franciscan 'Spirituals', partisans of extreme poverty. Some of these groups crossed openly into heresy: this was the case of the Waldenses, who took their name from Peter Waldo, a wealthy merchant of Lyons. The Waldenses broke completely with the Church and formed a sect in the north of Italy, later becoming part of the protestant reform.

3. The main medieval heresy was, however, that of the Cathari or Albigenses, the name being taken from Albi, a city in mediterranean France, which was one of its main fortresses. Catharism was a late growth of an old religious current, a mixture of gnostic and dualist elements, which had produced all sorts of sects in the Christian east, like the Paulicians and the Balkan Bogomils. Catharism was structured like a church; it had an inner group of the 'perfect', and a mass of mere adherents. Catharism was extremely successful among the people of Languedoc, being helped to this by sympathy shown it by the aristocracy, starting with the sovereign count of Toulouse, Raymond VI.

4. The papacy strove to deal with the Albigensian heresy by religious means, such as missions, in which St Dominic Guzman took part (he was then a canon of Osma). But these missions had little success, and the assassination of the pope's legate Peter of Castelnau decided Pope Innocent III to call a crusade against the Albigenses. In this crusade, religious movements and temporal interests both played a part: the southern nobility fought under the Albigensian banner to protect their lands from the greed of the northern barons, led by Simon of Montfort. The military victory of the crusade was completed by the Inquisition, which had been created to combat this heresy, the first heresy in the Christian middle ages to put roots down in the west.

5. It was the scale of this heresy which caused the establishment of the Inquisition, the institution designed specifically for the defence of the faith and the struggle against heresy. The ecclesiastical and civil authorities vied in their efforts in this direction. Emperor Frederick II — a great adversary of the papacy — issued an edict which laid down death by burning as punishment for the crime of heresy (1220). Pope Gregory IX, for his part, established the papal Inquisition (1232) whose function was to safeguard the faith (which was then regarded as the greatest treasure shared by the Christian people). However, inquisitional trials had serious defects which are an embarrassment to people nowadays; and the same is true of their system of penalties, with death as the punishment for the crime of heresy. The Inquisition had the misfortune to be a child of its time; it was born in a period when law was becoming stricter everywhere.

6. The lower middle ages saw the emergence of a new breed of heresy which is rightly considered pre-protestant. The writings of Wyclif, a professor of the University of Oxford, contain propositions which were condemned by the Church and which coincide with theses of the sixteenth-century reformers — the principle that sacred scripture is the only source of faith; the conception of the Church as an invisible 'community of the predestined'; the common priesthood of the faithful as the only priesthood; denial of the real presence of Christ in the Eucharist; bitter criticism of the papacy; etc.

7. Wyclif's teachings had a marked influence on the writings and preachings of John Huss, a priest and teacher at the University of Prague. Huss' ideas were well received in his own Bohemia. Denounced as a heretic, he tried to justify his position at the council of Constance; but he was condemned and died at the stake on 6 July 1415. His death made him a religious martyr and a national hero. In the Hussite wars Czechs confronted the empire and eventually a compromise was reached in the form of the *Compacts* of Basel: the moderate Hussites were allowed certain liturgical usages of their own, such as communion under both kinds (which was why they were called 'Utraquists'). On the eve of the reformation the Church in Bohemia, with its internal split between Catholics and Utraquists, represented a note of ambiguity unknown elsewhere in European Christendom.

18

The Crisis of Christendom

The serious clashes in the thirteenth century between the popes and the German emperors were the main factor responsible for the breakdown of the system of Christendom. A new secular spirit and a tendency towards ecclesiastical nationalism motivated the rulers of the great western monarchs. In its golden exile at Avignon, the papacy of the fourteenth century lived in the shadow of France.

1. The political and doctrinal system of Christendom suffered a crisis in the thirteenth century with the appearance of a new ideological and spiritual outlook in the Europe of the later middle ages. A main factor in this crisis was heated confrontation between papacy and empire, represented respectively by the popes who succeeded Innocent III, and the Hohenstaufen Emperor Frederick II. Frederick had assumed the imperial crown without relinquishing his sovereignty over Naples and Sicily, which made the pope very uneasy because it meant that the papal states were surrounded by German dominions. The personality of Frederick, which was closer to that of a renaissance prince than to that of a Christian emperor, and his suspect religious faith only increased the pope's apprehension. Gregory IX (1227-41) and Innocent IV (1243-54) were the great adversaries of Frederick II (+ 1250) in a war of unusual violence which divided Italy into two factions — the Guelphs, on the pope's side, and the Ghibellines, who supported the emperor. The popes gave the kingdom of Naples and Sicily to Charles of Anjou, who murdered the last members of the male line of the Staufen dynasty. A woman, Constance, transmitted the family's rights to her husband, Peter III of Aragon, and the Sicilian Vespers gave him the island of Sicily, which marked the beginning of Spanish presence in the south of Italy.

2. The violence of these struggles between papacy and empire dealt a mortal blow to the whole system of medieval Christendom. Other historical factors helped to hasten the process, for the decline of the empire coincided with the rise of other states, especially France, which became the secular power on whose support the papacy now had to rely. In these new circumstances, the self-assertion of the larger western kingdoms and the ecclesiastical nationalism that went with it undermined the necessary sense of unity which had inspired the political thinking behind Christendom. The crisis in the empire went so deep that on the death of Conrad IV (1254) the throne remained vacant for seventeen years – the so-called 'long interregnum'. But the papacy also suffered the consequences of the breakdown of the Christian ethnarchy: among the Germanic peoples resentment against Rome began to develop — distant rumbling of the Lutheran revolution; and in the Church itself an ardent desire could be felt for a more spiritual papacy and one less involved in worldly affairs.

3. The prophecies of the Cistercian abbot Joachim of Fiore, forecasting a new age of the Church, which would be ushered in by the election of an angelic pope, nourished these hopes for renewal. This climate of opinion, which obtained at the end of the thirteenth century, was reflected in the election to the papacy of Peter of Morrone, who took the name of Celestine V. But Celestine, conscious of his inability to govern the Church, resigned after five months. Benedict Gaetani, who succeeded him as Boniface VIII, was not so much an evangelical pastor as a jurist in love with the principle of papal supremacy. His pontificate marked the start of a series of crises, as dramatic and prolonged as any the Church has experienced in the twenty centuries of its history.

4. This era of crisis began with a clash between Boniface and the king of France, Philip the Fair. The pope was completely involved with the idea of the superiority of his apostolic authority, even in the temporal sphere, and he tried to behave like a latter-day Innocent III, but in very different historical circumstances. Philip the Fair was an able and unscrupulous politician, the first 'modern' king of the French monarchy. Boniface VIII issued the famous bull *Unam Sanctum* (18 November 1302) — the most complete exposition ever of pontifical theocracy — and demanded that the king accept this teaching. The conflict reached its climax when Guillaume of Nogaret, counsellor to the king, stormed Anagni, made the pope his prisoner and publicly confronted him. One month later Boniface died and the papacy, transplanted by Clement V from Rome to Avignon, became virtually under the control of France, for a long period, which came to be known as the Babylonian captivity.

5. In Avignon, the papacy became a French thing and lost its universality: the next seven popes were French, and so were ninety *per cent.* of the cardinals. The Avignon popes had a good reputation as administrators and they pursued the policy of centralisation of church government begun by the Gregorian reform; there was a steady growth in papal reserves, that is, appointments, grants, dispensations etc reserved to the pope. This centralisation increased the costs of running the Apostolic See, just at a time when income from the church states in Italy was decreasing alarmingly due to anarchy. These popes — especially John XXII (1316-34) — created the most advanced fiscal system of the time, seeking to maximise revenue from every possible source. The exchequer at Avignon was very successful in its efforts to exact tribute but at the cost of lowering the prestige of the papacy among those who paid this tribute. This unpopularity of the papacy would prove very harmful in the long run.

6. The Avignon period saw the emergence of famous anti-papal agitators, many of whom gathered at the court of the Emperor Louis IV of Bavaria during his long conflict with John XXII and his successors. At this court also, the leader of the 'Spiritualist' branch of the Franciscans sought asylum (these were at odds with the popes on the question of poverty); they included Michael of Cesena and the Englishman William of Ockham, who in his writings argued strongly in support of the role of the empire in the Christian world and proposed a democratic system of government for the Church, The most notorious member of Louis IV's entourage was Marsilius of Padua, previously rector of the University of Paris and author of *Defensor Pacis*, a work which he openly broke with Christian doctrinal tradition. For Marsilius, the pope enjoyed no special power and had only a priestly function; the hierarchy of the Church was a human creation; the Church had no power of jurisdiction and priests could receive such power only from princes; the Church, in other words, was absolutely dependent on the state.

7. *Defensor Pacis* represents the quintessence of doctrinaire anti-papalism. Without going to that extreme, a new secular spirit spread widely in the course of the fourteenth century. The reception of Roman law had the effect of strengthening kings' power and of preparing the way for the consolidation of national kingdoms. The agents of this policy were lay jurists, counsellors to kings, like the famous legists in the service of Philip the Fair of France. This new policy proclaimed the absolute sovereignty of the state, which in no way was dependent on the papacy; furthermore, the king's absolute power also extended to ecclesiastical affairs, favouring the nationalization of the Church in each kingdom. In England, the laws of *provisors* (1351) and of *praemunire* (1353, 1365 and 1393) helped decisively to create an Anglican church, well subject to the king long before Henry VIII and the reformation. In France, the secular spirit and the increase in the power of the monarchy were the source of the Gallicanism which culminated eventually in the Pragmatic Sanction of Bourges (1438); this formalized a particularism in the Church in France which endured until the French Revolution in the eighteenth century.

8. All the finer spirits of the time – from St Catherine of Siena or St Brigit to Petrarch – yearned for the return of the popes to Rome. The ground was prepared for this by the pacification of the papal states by Cardinal Gil de Albornoz. At last, Gregory XI (1370–8) resolved to leave Avignon and made his entry into Rome, in January 1377, to scenes of popular jubilation. It looked as if a sorry time was drawing to a close. But the time of testing was far from over: fourteen months later Gregory XI died and a new chapter began in the long crisis of the Church – the western schism.

19

The Western Schism and Conciliarism

The crisis in Christendom led to the western schism. The Christian kingdoms divided their obedience between two and even three popes, each claiming to be lawful head of the Church. In this climate of confusion, conciliarist doctrines tried to change the structure of church government, making the ecumenical council a court of final appeal, superior to the pope.

1. In the castle of Peniscola, which was the residence of Peter de Luna — Benedict XIII, as he is called in the list of Avignon popes during the schism — there is a stone inscription which leaves to the day of judgment the solution of the puzzle of the legitimacy or not of this man whose own firm belief was that he was pope. How could such uncertainty arise, which had such a dramatic impact on the Church? First we shall try to identify the facts, before any attempt to interpret them.

2. Two great protagonists played key roles in the origin of the western schism — the college of cardinals and the people of Rome. When it was called to elect in Rome a successor to Gregory XI, who had died shortly after his return from Avignon, the sacred college had a majority of French members, as had been the case throughout the Avignon period. The people of Rome fervently desired the election of an Italian pope, to avoid the danger of any new transfer of the papacy to Avignon. In an atmosphere of popular passion and riots in the streets, the conclave, on 8 April 1378, elected an Italian, Bartolomeo Prignano, archbishop of Bari, who took the name of Urban VI (1378-89). A few months later, the French majority in the sacred college left Rome and declared the papal election invalid on the grounds it had not been free because of the pressures exerted by the people of Rome. This majority group of cardinals met in Fondi in September of the same year and elected as pope one of their number, Cardinal Robert of Geneva, who took the name of Clement VII (1378–94). Clement established himself at Avignon, the two elected popes excommunicated each other, and the Church was in open schism.

3. The great problem was that the key to the legitimacy of one or other pope depended on something as difficult to assess as the validity of the election of Urban VI: did popular pressure so frighten the cardinals as to deprive them of freedom of choice and, therefore, render the election invalid? In other words, if the first election were valid, then Urban VI was the lawful pope; if not, then Clement VII was. It all depended on something as difficult to establish, with certainty, from outside, as the extent to which fear governed the voting of the sacred college. The confusion caused by the schism meant that Christendom was divided into two, with the kingdoms adhering to one or other 'obedience' — to the extent that even saints were divided, with St Catherine of Siena standing for Urban VI and St Vincent Ferrer promoting the obedience of Avignon.

4. The schism lasted a long time, with papal successions at both Rome and Avignon making it even more difficult to get a solution despite the strong desire for unity felt by the Christian people at large. In 1408, after thirty years had gone by, Gregory XII was pope in Rome and Benedict XIII — Peter de Luna — was at the head of the Avignon obedience. A group of Roman cardinals and another of Avignon's decided to hold a council in order in this way to bring the schism to an end. The council, which met in Pisa in 1409, declared deposed the two reigning popes and elected a new pope, Alexander V. But this election, far from solving anything, only added a new element of confusion: the popes at Rome and Avignon refused to abdicate, with the result that Christendom was now divided into not two but three obediences. A limit had been reached, and the idea grew that only a council of the whole Church could solve the crisis. This idea was taken up enthusiastically by the recently elected German emperor, Sigismund, whom the Pisa pope, John XXIII — the successor of Alexander V — authorized to call the ecumenical council of Constance.

5. Constance was a peculiar council, a sort of assembly of the Christian nations of Europe. Even its voting system was strange; there was not the normal counting of heads; instead a vote was assigned to each 'nation' — French, English, German, Italian and Spanish — and a further vote was given to the college of cardinals. But the most important step taken by this council occurred when Pope John XXIII — the first pope to bear this name —, on being invited to abdicate, refused to do so and fled from the city. The council then issued the decree *Sacrosancta* (6 April 1415) proclaiming itself the supreme arbiter of the catholic Church, with an authority received directly from Christ, and claiming that every authority, including that of the pope, was subject to it, in matters to do with faith, the schism or the reform of the Church. In this way, Constance made its own that conciliarist doctrine which affirmed that ecumenical councils were superior to the pope, thus changing the very foundations of the constitution of the Church.

6. The *Sacrosancta* decree can only be properly evaluated within the historical context in which it was issued: that is, after a century of crisis in the Church, and forty years of schism. It is true that conciliarist theories had been professed by arch anti-papalists like Ockham and Marsilius; but the conciliarist arguments also drew support from the great masses of texts assembled in the codexes of collections of the *Corpus juris canonici*, the 'decretists' and 'decretalists' echoed the thousands of hypotheses based on all possible suppositions which had been debated in the schools — naturally, on the level of pure theory. The novelty lay in the fact that it was not a matter now of academic *questiones disputatae*: serious concrete problems needed to be solved. This explains why the conciliarist doctrine got such a good reception, especially among French and German academics, with the chancellor of the University of Paris, Jean Gerson, to the fore.

7. The conciliarist doctrine of the *Sacrosancta* decree established the superior authority of ecumenical councils in the Church. But the council of Constance was not satisfied with formulating this doctrine on the level of principles; it tried to establish a permanent system whereby it would be normal for synods to take part in the supreme government of the Church. This was the purpose of its *Frequens* decree (9 October 1417) which made the ecumenical council a permanent institution in the Church: another council would be held in five years' time, another seven years later and then others every ten years — automatically, without any need of being convoked by the pope. Having thus topped out the conciliarist restructuring of the Church, the council then proceeded to the election of a pope by the cardinals present at Constance, with six additional electors, one from each of the conciliar 'nations.' Cardinal Oddo Colonna was elected with the name of Martin V (11 November 1417) and was recognized by all Christendom: the western schism had come to an end.

8. The council of Constance had succeeded in putting an end to the schism; but its conciliarist decrees were justly suspect and the new pope, Martin V, did not confirm them. It was inevitable that sooner or later there would be a confrontation between the papacy and doctrinaire conciliarism, to decide on whether pope or council was supreme. The clash took place during the pontificate of Eugene IV (1431-47), at the council of Basle. This council, which began with total legality, was radicalized to the point of becoming an assembly of clergy, with only a minimum representation of bishops. Those present at the council eventually broke with the pope, declared him deposed, and elected as anti-pope Duke Amadeus of Savoy, a peculiar individual, who took the name of Felix V. Eugene IV replied by condemning the 'conventicle' of Basle and its conciliarist doctrine. Abandoned by all the Christian kingdoms, the schismatic group which formed the rump of the council fell apart. And so the crisis of conciliarism came to an end with a clear reaffirmation of the Roman primacy.

20

Between the Middle Ages and the Modern Period

A whole series of factors brought about the transition from the middle ages to the modern period. A man-created view of the world and enthusiasm over pagan antiquity shaped the hearts and minds of the élites, whereas the people in general remained faithful to their religious traditions and the devotio moderna *enriched Christian piety. No general ecclesiastical reform took place. The renaissance popes were great patrons of the arts. Constantinople — the second Rome — fell to the Turks; but the discovery of America opened up a new continent to the gospel.*

1. Light and shadow, hopes and failures — a whole cumulation of contradictory factors seemed to flow together during the period of transition between the middle ages and the modern period. An ambiguity hung over this period, a question-mark about the future and about the meaning of the new age which, according to all the indications, was about to begin. The fifteenth century and the dawn of the sixteenth form the gateway to the modern age, and they produced two phenomena whose immense importance would condition all future history — the invention of printing, an incomparable instrument for the spread of ideas, and the discovery of America, which opened up a new continent to the gospel.

2. In the period between the middle of the fifteenth century and the year 1517 — covering approximately two generations — saw a change, from well-founded hopes of a full restoration of Christian unity, to the drama of religious division running right through western Christendom. The popes of the fifteenth century aspired to bring the eastern schism to an end, and the finest men in the Greek Church felt this same desire. The Turkish menace threatening Constantinople inclined the rulers of the Byzantine empire to draw closer to the Christian west. The ecumenical council of Ferrara-Florence was a great unionist council. Present at it were the emperor, John VIII, and seven hundred representatives of the eastern patriarchates and of the Russian Church. All questions of discipline and doctrine (including the *Filioque*) which separated the eastern churches from the catholic Church were debated in the presence of pope and emperor and, finally, on 6 July 1439, the bull of union *Laetentur caeli* was solemnly proclaimed — and in succeeding years a number of other Christian confessions in the east accepted it.

3. But the triumph of Christianity was more apparent than real and it soon ended in tragedy. When John VIII returned to Constantinople he did not dare make the union public, out of fear of the people's reaction, and Russia openly withdrew from the Florence agreement. Eventually, on 12 December 1452, Constantine XI, John VIII's successor, decided to proclaim the union of the Churches, despite violent hostility from anti-Latin fanatics. But the days of Byzantium were numbered. Six months later, on 29 May 1453, Constantinople fell to the Turks and the Christian empire of the east perished. With it disappeared that goal, so long desired, of the unity of the eastern churches with Rome, just when it seemed to have been reached. The east having been lost, the other great drama of modern Christendom began to unfold at the beginning of the sixteenth century and the Church would lose half of the peoples of the European west.

4. The fifteenth century witnessed some events which promised much for the future of Christianity: the popes were living at Rome once more, the eastern schism was at an end, the fog of conciliarism had cleared. But the impulse was lacking for that spiritual renewal essential for the 'reform of the Church in its head and in its members' which people everywhere were calling for. Some partial efforts were made, such as the ecclesiastical reform brought about in Spain by the catholic monarchs. But there was no general movement of this type, which explains why the catholic reformation came after the protestant reformation. An impetus for general renewal could only come from its supreme authority, the Roman papacy, but unfortunately the renaissance popes from the 1450's onwards — magnificent patrons of the arts — were more temporal princes than pastors devoted to the care of the faithful, who so needed that care in view of the culture in which they lived, at the beginning of the modern age.

5. In the inventory of lights and shadows which formed a sequence during this transition period, one indubitable fact is that the people continued to be deeply religious and Christian. The lower middle ages did not have that creativity of the great age of Christendom, but that is not to say that they had nothing of spiritual value. Mysticism flourished — especially in the German countries of the Rhine — with such great names as Eckhart and Tauler, Suso and Ruysbroeck. At a popular level, the *devotio moderna* nourished a more personal and more interior type of piety, whose spirit reflects Thomas à Kempis' *Imitation of Christ*. But even spiritual life showed signs of dangerous imbalance: for example, there was an obsession with death, an aftermath of the Black Death of 1347-52 and other later epidemics. This subject inspired the painting of the dance of death, and the liturgy of the dead gained the beautiful *Dies irae* sequence. Even the reformist enthusiasm of Savonarola suffered from this terribly sombre note.

6. The theology of the fourteenth and fifteenth centuries did little for intellectual life. Traditional theology, in the form of decadent scholasticism, seemed empty and unoriginal. It was the 'old way' and, in successful opposition to it, there arose the 'modern way', represented especially by the nominalism of William of Ockham. For nominalism, the inner mind can reach only what is individual and visible to the senses, so that universal concepts are nothing but words — *nomina*. Nominalism was fideistic, for according to it revelation is the only route to knowing the more essential religious truths, such as the existence of God and the immortality of the soul. Its exaggerated divine voluntarism endangered the basis of morality: actions were not good or bad by their very nature: it was just that God commanded them or prohibited them. Thus, nominalist theology offered a very unsure foundation for the doctrinal and religious turmoil which was in the offing.

7. But the transition from the middle ages to the modern ages was dominated, above all, by two great cultural phenomena which really shaped the spirit of the period — the renaissance and humanism. They were, naturally, minority movements, the preserve of select groups, but they were to exercise an enduring influence on the history of the European west. The renaissance, filled with enthusiasm for Greek and Roman antiquity, also adopted the ideas of that culture, and this had a strong paganizing effect on people's outlook . A sense of worldliness meant that earthly life was given pride of place. Instead of God being seen as the centre of things, now man was the leading actor, the measure of all things.

8. Humanism consisted in passionate cultivation of the Greek and Latin classics as a source of the culture and wisdom of the ancient world. The humanists rejected what they called the barbarism of medieval scholasticism and proposed a learned piety, largely the fruit of combining Christianity with the best elements of antiquity. The Academia Platonica, created in the Florence of Lorenzo the Magnificent by Marsilio Ficino (1433-99) aimed at a Christian renaissance based on Plato and Cicero, the sermon on the mount and St Paul. The most outstanding of the humanists was Desiderius Erasmus (1466-1536) who did so much for biblical studies and historical criticism. But his 'philosophy of Christ' was a non-dogmatic Christianity, barely anything more than a moral system. Erasmus was zealous, after his fashion, for the reform of the Church, but his was a bitter zeal, given to destructive criticism, which did more harm than good. However, outside of Spain, where the humanism shaped by Cardinal Cisneros was sincerely Christian, the religious legacy of the humanists, made no great contribution to the hoped-for reform of the Church.

21

The Reformation in Germany:
Luther and Lutheranism

*Martin Luther was the soul of the great religious revolution which broke
the unity of western Christianity. Luther's complex personality galvanized
long-standing German resentment of Rome and nicely suited the ambitions
of the German princes.*

1. Martin Luther was the author of the protestant reformation;
however, although this former Augustinian friar had a remarkable
personality and great leadership qualities, his success as a reformer
was also due, to a considerable degree, to a   combination of opportune
circumstances. Luther had a great ability to interpret ideas and feelings
widespread in the Germany of his time and to deliver answers which
satisfied the religious aspirations of some and the political ambitions
of others. The sheer speed with which the flame of the reformation
spread is a good indication that the wind was blowing in its favour,
that time was ripe. Therefore, to understand the origin and
development of Lutheranism we must first look at the historical
background.

2. Many of the germs which helped spread the Lutheran revolution
had been in the air for some time past. The whole process of the
breakdown of the principles and attitudes on which medieval
Christendom was based was at the same time a preparation for the
reformation — the conciliarist doctrines, the movement for democracy
in the Church, nominalist philosophy, the pressures exerted on its
tributaries by the Avignon exchequer, the western schism. Political
factors, also, played their part — for example, the clashes between
popes and emperors and the rise of ecclesiastical nationalism. And
there were other causes, to do with specifically German circumstances
— moral decadence of the clergy and especially of the episcopacy,
which was the virtual monopoly of the nobility; the weakness of
sovereign power in an empire fragmented into innumerable
principalities and cities, and especially resentment towards Rome,

which in the previous century had taken the concrete form in *Gravamina Germanicae nationis*, a catalogue of grievances of the German nations against the Roman curia. All these factors combined to create a climate ripe for a deep religious crisis.

3. Martin Luther, as we were saying, was able to personify the feelings of many Germans of his time. But that does not mean that he had not a religious motivation which had a strong influence on his mental itinerary and his external activity. From the time he became a friar, Luther worried anxiously over how to be sure of being saved. The Ockhamist theology in which he had been trained, while proclaiming the arbitrary voluntarism of God, held that man's free will alone was all that was needed for fulfilling God's law and reaching heaven. Father Martin felt that this doctrine was quite at odds with his own experience: he felt incapable of overcoming concupiscence by his own efforts alone, and of achieving through his own efforts the assurance of salvation he so yearned for. Meditation on verse 17 of the first chapter of the Letter to the Romans — 'He who through faith is righteous shall live' — was how Luther found a way out of his acute anxiety. He believed he understood that merciful God justifies man through faith ('fiducial faith') and in the light of this principle it seemed to him that all scripture took on a new meaning.

4. On this foundation — the real axiom of his 'theology of consolation' — Luther built a doctrinal system in open contradiction to the tradition of the Church. Human nature, according to him, has been completely corrupted by sin. Justification is something which springs from man's 'fiducial', trusting, faith: it is not an interior healing of man but a declaration by God graciously clothing him with the merits of Christ's death. A man's works are of no avail for his salvation: the ministerial priesthood does not have any reason for being, nor do the majority of the sacraments, or monastic vows, or, especially, the papacy, the worst invention of Antichrist. Luther devised a purely interior conception of the Church and rejected any constitutional element in the Church — particularly, canon law. The Church, therefore, does not hold the deposit, is not the interpreter of, revelation: 'scripture alone' is, according to Luther, the only source of revelation, and it is up to each Christian to interpret it, inspired directly by God.

5. Luther did not formulate this doctrine overnight; he did it gradually, becoming ever bolder, and getting further and further away from catholic orthodoxy. His immense success can be partly attributed to the favourable combination of circumstances to which we have referred; but there were other more immediate factors. First among these was the extraordinary personality of the reformer himself — full of contradictions, yet quite overpowering — which combined obsessive religiosity and tender piety towards Jesus Christ with an earthiness which took its coarsest form in his diatribes against the pope.

6. Luther's teachings were accepted by different people for different reasons. His suppression of celibacy was welcomed by many priests, at a time when the moral level of the clergy was quite low; and his suppression of monastic vows sounded a liberty bell for monks and nuns whose fervour had grown cold. His 'theology of consolation', according to which faith without works brought justification, made Christian life easier and tranquilized people who though conscious of their sins nevertheless had religious feelings and were anxious to save their souls. Lutheran anti-Romanism pleased humanists like Ulrich von Hutten; and, particularly, the chance of taking over ecclesiatical property enticed the greed of the princes and even of the holders of authority in certain imperial cities. It must be added that Luther had a marvellous flair for propaganda; he took maximum advantage of the printing press and flooded Germany with booklets, hymnbooks and broadsheets which gave everyone access to his teaching.

7. We should trace, very briefly, the main lines of the German reformation process starting with the year 1517. The Dominicans were preaching indulgences to raise funds for the building of St Peter's; Martin Luther, an Augustinian friar and teacher at Wittenberg, reacted against this, publishing ninety-seven theses against scholastic theology (4 September 1517) and sending on 31 October 1517 to the archbishop of Mainz ninety-five theses on indulgences. In the years that followed Luther's became a household name. When called to Rome he refused to go and instead attended the imperial diets at Augsburg (1518) and Leipzig (1519), each time adopting a more critical attitude to the Church. Rome took no decisive action against him, mainly for reasons of political opportunism: the empire was vacant and the candidate preferred by Pope Leo was Elector Frederick the Wise of Saxony, in whose territory Luther lived and who was Luther's great patron. When Charles V was elected emperor (1519) Luther published three famous items, which implied his open break with the Church — *An appeal to the nobility of the German nation, On the Babylonian captivity of the Church,* and his

Liberty of a Christian man. He was eventually excommunicated in 1521.

8. At the Diet of Worms, Charles V and Martin Luther met face to face. 'I neither can nor will recant anything', declared the former friar. The insight of that young emperor (he was only twenty-one) was quite remarkable; in one day he sized up the situation and realized the seriousness of the religious revolt (the Roman curia took ages to come to the same conclusion). That very night Charles produced in his own handwriting a document which on the following day, 19 April 1521, he presented to the diet, proclaiming his resolve 'to employ my kingdom and my lordships, my friends, my body, my blood, my life and my soul' to fight heresy and to defend the catholic faith. Only death brought an end to this struggle between the author of the reformation and the last great Christian emperor of Europe.

9. Lutheranism took over principalities and cities with great speed. In the social upheaval of the Peasants' War Luther took the side of the princes and exhorted them to assume ecclesiastical authority in their territories. Lutheranism consolidated its position in the political as well as in the theological sphere: the princes and cities of the reform formed a confessional league, and Melanchton fixed Lutheran doctrine in the Confession of Augsburg (1530). A year earlier, the diet of Speyer granted toleration to the reform in those territories where it was already established, but prohibited its spread to new territories. The protest of five states and fourteen cities coined a new name: Protestants, Protestantism.

10. When Luther died in 1546, the reformation had spread over more than half of Germany. In the same year the council of Trent began, fifteen years after Charles V had called for it. In 1547, the conflict between the emperor and the protestant princes degenerated into armed warfare and Charles obtained a complete victory over the Schmalkaldic league at Mühlberg. But later the treachery of Maurice of Saxony obliged the emperor to grant religious freedom to the Lutherans (the treaty of Passau, 1552). In 1555, Charles, now tired and aged, and on the point of retiring, had to sanction the peace of Augsburg, which gave equal rights to Catholics and Lutherans, with it being left to each prince to decide which confession should be followed in his territory: *cujus regio ejus religio.* The religious division of Germany was now an accomplished and irreversible fact.

22

The Protestant Reformation in Europe

The protestant revolt separated half of the people of Europe from the Church. It took different forms. Protestantism – Lutheran or Calvinist in inspiration – became the state religion in most of the countries of central and northern Europe. Anglicanism was a schism, which became protestantized after Henry VIII.

1. Germany was the first scenario of the religious revolution begun by Luther, but it did not stay within the frontiers of the empire. The seeds of the reformation were soon blown over the greater part of the European west. The rapid spread of Protestantism was quite remarkable, whether it happened in the form of Lutheranism or in other, different forms, all of which involved breaking with catholic orthodoxy. After dominating more than half of Germany, the protestant revolt separated from the trunk of the Church half of the peoples who had made up medieval Christendom. We will now look at the more salient features of this phenomenon which changed the face of continental Europe.

2. Lutheranism took over the Scandinavian countries fairly easily; their rulers quickly broke with Rome, confiscated the Church's property and created their national churches. In German Switzerland, Zwingli (1484–1531), a priest at Galrus, in 1518 started his own religious revolt, whose radicalism enraged Luther himself: he regarded Zwingli as an 'unchristian man', particularly because of his doctrine that Christ was only symbolically present in the Eucharist. But in terms of importance, the second great figure in the reformation, for both his doctrinal contribution and his influence on the progress of Protestantism, was John Calvin.

3. Calvin (1509-64), who was born in Noyon in France and embraced Protestantism from his early years, opened up new avenues for Protestantism. Endowed with a more logical and rigorous mind than Luther's, Calvin brought the basic premises of Protestantism to their logical limits. In his judgment, Luther's theology of consolation was quite inadequate. Man's utter corruption and God's absolute voluntarism led inevitably to the Calvinist doctrine of predestination. God — transcendent and incomprehensible — by his inscrutable decision predestines people to heaven or hell, extending salvation to some, damnation to others. The true church is the congregation of the predestined — *coetus praedestinorum*; from which it followed that it is interior and invisible. But there is also a visible church, composed of the assembly of the faithful incorporated into it by baptism and sharing in the eucharistic supper, the only two sacraments which Calvin admitted. However, the very corruption of human nature demands that man be subjected to a life of strict morality, sobriety and hard work. This kind of life God will bless with prosperity in temporal affairs, a sign of God's favour and of predestination. Calvin's doctrine had a marked influence on the rise of modern capitalism.

4. Calvin spelt out his doctrine in his treatise *Institutes of the Christian Religion* which he wrote first in Latin and then expanded in a French version published in 1539. In Geneva, where he settled, Calvin established a quasi-theocratic régime and an austere form of social life, inspired by the laws of the Bible. Calvin was the religious autocrat governing the community, with the backing of a consistory made up of pastors and elders. The Theological Academy of Geneva was the seminary where he trained pastors to be sent to the various Calvinist communities of Europe. Geneva was vigilant in maintaining the purity of the reformed Christianity and the celebrated Spanish doctor Michael Servetus was condemned as a heretic and burned at the stake for denying the mystery of the Blessed Trinity.

5. Calvinist Protestantism spread much farther afield than Lutheranism (which was almost confined to Germany and the Scandinavian countries) and it had a decisive influence on the Christian destinies of Europe. In the centre and east of the continent, it put down deep roots in Hungary and Bohemia and won over part of the Polish aristocracy. In the Low Countries, William the Silent, Prince of Orange, became the protestant leader in the struggle against Philip II and the Catholics, and succeeded in establishing a sort of Calvinist fortress in the United Provinces of the north — the future Holland. In Scotland, Calvinism took the form of Presbyterianism: John Knox became the effective ruler of the country, from which the luckless Queen Mary Stuart fled to seek refuge in England.

Calvinism was also the dominant form of Protestantism in Calvin's own country of origin, France.

6. During the early stages of the reformation the French kings followed a religious policy of their own. From the time of Francis I, France was the constant ally of the German princes in their struggle against Charles V, and also of the Turks, who were threatening the eastern frontiers of the empire. It kept to the same line in the next century, in the decisive test of the Thirty Years War. But in internal politics, the French kings normally conducted themselves as faithful Catholics, and both Francis I and Henry II acted with severity towards their protestant subjects. But Calvinism did make its way in France, counting many aristocrats among its number, and it was not long before two major factions emerged, one catholic, led by the Guises, and the other protestant, whose most famous leaders where Admiral de Coligny and the Bourbon prince, Henry of Navarre. The regent, Catherine de Médici, the widow of Henry II, tried to remain neutral and cool the situation. But she failed, and France was plunged into wars of religion for almost three decades. The St Bartholomew's Day massacre and the assassination of the duke de Guise and of Henry II were the most outstanding events in this anguished period of civil war.

7. The history of the reformation in England followed a course of its own and, perhaps more than in any other country, went where the monarchy led it. As we have said already, Anglicanism was not an invention of Henry VIII. In the fifteenth century the Church in England was already in a certain sense an Anglican Church and Henry VIII found in the ecclesiastical legislation of his predecesors devices suitable to his policy of subjection of Church to state. In his youth this prince had been the champion of Catholicism at the dawn of the reformation; he wrote a *Defence of the seven sacraments* against Luther, for which Leo X confered on him the title of Defender of the Faith, *Defensor fidei*. It was the Pope's refusal to allow him to divorce his wife Catherine of Aragon to marry Anne Boleyn that provoked Henry to reject the Roman primacy and enter into schism. But schism — not Protestantism — was as far as the reformation went in England while Henry lived. He proclaimed himself 'supreme head of the Church of England' and required sworn recognition of his ecclesiastical supremacy. The great majority of churchmen timidly submitted to the king's will. But there were admirable exceptions, such as the Carthusian martyrs and especially two outstanding personalities who refused to conform and died for the faith — St John

Fisher, bishop of Rochester, and St Thomas More, lord chancellor of the kingdom and the finest humanist in England, an exemplary family man, a Christian who is attractive and modern even today.

8. A calvinistic Protestantism was introduced into England during the reign of Edward VI (1547-53). His successor Mary Tudor, the daughter of Henry VIII and Catherine of Aragon, repressed the heresy and tried to restore Catholicism. But this restoration lasted only the few short years of her reign (1553-58). When she died childless, the crown passed to Elizabeth, the daughter of Henry VIII and Anne Boleyn. Elizabeth's long reign decided the fate of English Christianity. The external forms of the catholic tradition were kept, such as the hierarchy with its bishops and cathedral chapters, although without clerical celibacy or monastic life. The celebration of Mass was outlawed and a protestantized Anglicanism, containing Lutheran and Calvinist elements, was imposed as the official teaching of the Church of England.

23

The Catholic Reformation

Eager desires for Christian renewal led to a great flourishing in the Church itself; in some places this began before the advent of Lutheranism. Old religious orders were reformed, new ones were founded, great saints and great popes appeared. The council of Trent did not obtain the objective so desired by Charles V of restoring Christian unity; but it did achieve an enormous amount in the area of catholic doctrine and church discipline.

1. The catholic reformation, as a movement of renewal in the universal Church fostered by the papacy, began later than the protestant reformation. But the desire for reform was there much earlier and already had produced some important results, though they did not affect the whole Church. The forerunner of the catholic reformation was the Spain of the catholic kings. Ferdinand and Isabella regarded church reform as an essential part of their own primary objective, the restoration of the Spanish state. The right of presentation which they obtained, first for the bishoprics of the reconquered kingdom of Granada and later for almost all the sees in the country, enabled them to take the episcopate out of the hands of the nobility and choose as bishops, men eminent for their religious spirit and education, many of them drawn from the regular clergy. Cardinal Cisneros reformed the Franciscan convents and monastic life; the University of Alcalá, founded by him, was a great centre of theological studies (which published the famous Complutensian Polyglot Bible), and an active focus of Christian humanism. The Spanish church in the first third of the sixteenth century was undoubtedly the best in Europe in terms of scientific and spiritual level, which explains the predominant role played by Spanish theologians at the council of Trent.

2. In Italy also there was in the same period a strong desire for Christian renewal. The Oratory of Divine Love began there, as a fraternity of enlightened and pious clergy and laity. Some of its members (Cajetan of Thiene and Giovanni Paolo Caraffa), convinced that a raising of the spiritual level was a pre-requisite to genuine reform, fostered the idea of regular clerics, that is, priests who would live in community and take the three religious vows, but without wearing a habit or attending choir, as was the case with monks and friars. This was the origin of the Theatines (1524), the first of these new bodies, who were followed by the Barabites (1530), the Somaschi and others. The work of spiritual renewal of clergy and of people spearheaded in Spain by St John of Avila was another important chapter in the religious history of the sixteenth century.

3. The most important religious foundation of the sixteenth century was undoubtedly that of the Society of Jesus by St Ignatius Loyola (1491-1556). Ignatius, along with five companions, took religious vows in Paris, and all six committed themselves to go on pilgrimage to Jerusalem and to consecrate their lives to the service of souls (1534). Finding it impossible to get to the Holy Land, they agreed to stay together and to place themselves, through a fourth vow, at the complete disposition of the pope. In 1540, Paul III approved the Society of Jesus as an order of regular clerics whose primary purpose was to spread catholic faith and teaching. The society developed rapidly: by the time its founder died it had a thousand members, and 13,000 half a century later. The Jesuits — as they came to be called — rendered great service to the papacy in its work of catholic reform, especially through training of the clergy, education of youth, and missions abroad.

4. This impulse of spiritual renewal, which continued right through the sixteenth century, also affected the old religious orders. In Spain, the reform of the Franciscans was led by St Peter of Alcántara, and that of the Benedictines by Abbot García de Cisneros. The reform of the Carmelites was brought about by St Teresa of Ávila (1515-82), and St John of the Cross extended it to the monks of that order. In Italy the Capuchins arose, as a new branch of the Franciscans, achieving great popularity on account of their austerity of life and dedication to the ministry.

5. The central event of the catholic reformation was, however, the council of Trent and its meeting marks the point at which the papacy at last took charge of the whole process of church renewal. To get the council going was itself no small task: a pre-conciliar period lasting fifteen long years was marked by vacillation, hopes and jealousy. The first voices calling for a council were raised in Germany, when the

Lutheran revolt, already in full swing, had opened the seam of religious division. Protestants as well as Catholics clamoured for a 'free, Christian council, on German soil.' Naturally, demands of this kind made Rome apprehensive: that sort of council sounded ambiguous, and the papacy feared a new growth of conciliarism, with its pretensions to make the council superior to the pope. Charles V was very anxious to see the council meet, hoping that it would help re-establish religious unity in the empire. But this perspective and the implications of any strengthening of Charles' power were enough to make the other great catholic king, Francis I of France, who was almost continuously at war with the emperor, not in the least enthusiastic about the convoking of the council.

6. The pope, Paul III (1534-49), knew very well that an ecumenical council was the only way to advance reform of the Church. And gradually all the many obstacles in the way of holding it were overcome. The choice of Trent as the location of the council was one of the compromises arrived at: Trent was in the north of Italy; but it was an imperial city and there was room for hope that the Protestants would agree to go there, whereas they would never take part in a council held on papal soil. Even the agenda for the council gave rise to differences of opinion: the pope wanted dogmatic questions to be dealt with first, in order to establish catholic dogma on the questions controverted by the Protestants; whereas the emperor wanted to see matters of church discipline dealt with first, hoping that this would satisfy his Lutheran subjects and help restore Christian unity. The compromise arrived at on this subject was that both matters would be dealt with at the same time, alternating dogmatic decrees with disciplinary ones. But the difficulties did not end with the opening of the council; in fact so many serious incidents arose in the course of its meeting that it was feared it would founder.

7. We cannot detail here all these incidents; we will simply mark the main chapters in the council's career. It was inaugurated on 13 December 1545, too late, of course, for there to be any real chance of its being a unionist council, with Protestants involved. On 11 March 1547, the papal legates, ostensibly out of fear of an epidemic, decided to transfer the council to Bologna, but their real reason was that they wanted to move the assembly out of reach of the emperor's influence, who was no longer on good terms with the pope; it is enough to recall that Charles's victory over the Lutherans at Mühlberg was received more with fear than with joy at the Roman curia. During the Bologna stage those bishops who were Charles' subjects did not attend but stayed at Trent. Finally, in January 1548, Charles made a formal protest which caused the council sessions at Bologna to cease and then led the suspension of the council in September 1549.

8. The second stage of the council opened in Trent on 1 May 1551, under the new pope, Julius III (1550-5). The emperor now managed to get a certain number of delegations from protestant cities and princes to attend. The presence of the reformers made it clear how difficult restoration of unity would be, after more than thirty years of religious division. In any event, the treachery of Elector Maurice of Saxony against Charles caused the council to be suspended once more (28 April 1552). This interruption lasted ten years, which covered the entire pontificate of Paul IV (1555-9), a zealous reformer, but in other ways than through the council. The third stage lasted only two years, which was enough to bring this great undertaking to a happy conclusion: on 4 December 1563 the council of Trent was closed and the pope confirmed all its decrees in his bull *Benedictus Deus*, 26 January 1564.

9. Trent was unable to be a unionist council; but it was the great council of the catholic reformation. It did an extraordinary amount of work, in the fields of both dogma and discipline. In dogma, it declared, above all, that divine revelation has been transmitted by sacred scripture — interpreted by the magisterium of the Church — and Apostolic tradition. The council tackled the key question of justification and, against the Calvinist and Lutheran theologies, declared that divine grace and the free and meritorious cooperation of the human will work together in the justification of man. The other subject of a dogmatic character dealt with by the council was that of the sacraments, where so much confusion had been sown by the Protestants: the doctrine of the seven sacraments was defined and the characteristics proper to each specified.

10. In the area of discipline the council also did important work. It made every effort to suppress the abuses that existed in the life of the Church, with the aim of ensuring the most effective pastoral care of the Christian people. An episcopacy fully dedicated to its ministry and a well-trained clergy   with a high standard of morality were goals of tridentine legislation. Bishops and parish priests were required to reside where their work placed them; the accummulation of benefices were prohibited; it was laid down that provincial councils and diocesan synods should meet periodically; and pastoral visitation was urged. The training — both intellectual and spiritual — of the clergy would take place in a seminary, which each diocese must have; and priests in their respective parishes had to catechise the children and give religious instruction to the faithful. This, in broad outline, was the reforming work of the council of Trent, which is even impressive to look at from this distance; but what is perhaps more remarkable still is the fact that this great movement of Christian renewal did not remain a dead letter but was put into practice in the period that followed the council.

24

From the Wars of Religion to the Final Split

The religious map of Europe was not finally drawn until well into the second half of the seventeenth century. Catholics and Protestants fought wars of religion in France. The dynamism of Trent led to Catholics regaining 'lost ground' in central Europe. In literature and art, the baroque was a faithful reflection of the spirit of post-tridentine Catholicism. But the decisive test was the Thirty Years War, in which the catholic Habsburg kingdoms confronted the protestant powers and their ally, France. The treaty of Westphalia fixed the final religious division of Europe. And in England, the Glorious Revolution led by William of Orange frustrated the pro-catholic leanings of the last of the Stuarts.

1. The period following the holding of the council of Trent was marked by the great renewal of catholic life which that council initiated. Reform went ahead, based on the tridentine constitutions and decrees and vigorously promoted by successive popes. A Roman catechism, a missal and a breviary were published by order of Pope St Pius V (1566-72). Gregory XIII (1572-85) entrusted to nuncios the task of overseeing the execution of the council decrees, and in Rome his successor, Sixtus V (1585-90), completely overhauled the Roman curia, which managed the central government of the Church.

2. The tridentine spirit led to the appearance of exemplary bishops who strove to apply the conciliar decrees on discipline of clergy and faithful. Their prototype was St Charles Borromeo, who, after working as a very young man as cardinal secretary of state to his uncle Pius IV, became a very zealous archbishop of Milan. In Rome itself, St Philip Neri (1515-95) did an enormous amount to renew the Christian life among members of the curia, through his work of spiritual direction and through his foundation of the Congregation of the Oratory. Also in Rome, St Joseph Calasanctius (1556-1648) worked with great self-denial at the Christian education of young people of the poorer classes, founding for them the Piarist schools. St Francis de Sales (1567-1622) fostered personal piety — the 'devout life' — among lay people living in the middle of the world.

3. The baroque was the artistic style of the catholic reformation. Architecture, sculpture, painting all served as a channel of expression of the baroque — in Spain, Italy, the catholic countries of central Europe and Hispanic America. Baroque Catholicism also inspired literature, and one of its most notable expressions was the *autos sacramentales*, theatrical pieces on a theological theme, a very good reflection of the Spanish spirit in the seventeenth century; the fact that these *autos* were understood by and were popular with the public at large is a good indication of the generally high level of religious knowledge.

4. As a result of the geographical discoveries of the fifteenth and sixteenth centuries the overseas horizons of Christianity had expanded enormously. St Francis Xavier had brought the gospel to Japan, and China also opened its door to missionaries. But the Portuguese possessions in Africa and Asia were the main areas of evangelization in these two continents, royal patronage being the key factor in ecclesiastical organization; the same thing happened in Brazil, the great Portuguese colony on the other shore of the Atlantic.

5. The main areas where Christianity spread was the immense Spanish empire of America and the far east. Particularly after Trent, the Spanish monarchy became very conscious of its role as a 'missionary state' and did much to consolidate earlier missionary work. The Spanish crown exercised a royal privilege, granted by Julius II in 1508, to nominate holders of bishoprics and other high ecclesiastical offices. Advances in education accompanied the spread of the gospel: while Trent was being held, three universities were already operating in the Indies: Santo Domingo (founded in 1538), Lima (1551) and Mexico (1553). Although it had many defects and abuses, on balance the work done by Spain and Portugal was positive: the indigenous peoples were respected and survived in freedom; they received Christian faith and culture, and today the hundreds of millions of Catholics in Latin America and the Philippines form the great demographic reserve of Christianity and the Church. The growing importance given in the Holy See to this whole missionary effort led to the establishment in 1622 of the Congregation of *Propaganda Fide*.

6. The thrust given by Trent led to other initiatives, such as the formation, by Pope St Pius V, of the Holy League, a veritable crusade against the Turks, which defeated them at the battle of Lepanto. Much lost ground was regained for Catholicism in central Europe. St Francis de Sales' missions in the Chablais area won back most of French Switzerland. Similar permanent gains were made in Austria and Bavaria, and in Poland and Bohemia. And the end of the wars of religion in France meant that that country stayed catholic despite its huguenot minority. In the east of Europe the Union of Brest (1596) saw a considerable part of the Orthodox hierarchy adhere to Catholicism and was the origin of the Ruthenian or Ukrainian uniate church.

7. All this movement towards catholic reform was actively fostered by the two great powers ruled by the house of Habsburg — Spain and the empire. Protestantism, now on the defensive, was afraid of a catholic reconquest of Germany, and the conflict (both religious and political) which was sparked off by the election of Ferdinand II as emperor ended in armed warfare. The Thirty Years War (1618-48) reduced the population of Germany by half and at one point the two catholic powers seemed to be on the point of complete victory. But just then another catholic power, France, stepped in and tipped the balance in favour of the protestant princes. Paradoxically, this was a France governed by famous cardinals — Richelieu (+1642), Mazarin (+1661) — and it must be recognized that they did attain their objectives: Spain ceased to be supreme in Europe, the empire was severely weakened and the Habsburg encirclement of France collapsed. Indeed, France became the premier power in Europe. But these successes, achieved in the treaty of Westphalia, were expensive in religious terms: the advance of the catholic reconquest in Germany was blocked, and the renewed hopes of a return to Christian unity faded. Modern Europe, which really began at Westphalia, was born with a divided soul, and once again the principle of *cujus regio ejus religio* — let each state follow the religion of the prince — confirmed the confessional fragmentation of a Germany made up of 343 principalities and cities. The ideal of European Christendom was no more.

8. In the basilica of St Peter there are two tombs which seem to symbolize the hopes and frustrations of the seventeenth century — the tombs of Christina of Sweden and of the last of the Stuarts. Queen Christina, the daughter and heir of Gustavus Adolphus, the protestant hero of the Thirty Years War, became a Catholic in 1654; but she renounced the throne and moved to Rome, where she lived for the rest of her life. The restoration of the Stuarts in England and Scotland, after the puritan republican dictatorship of Oliver Cromwell, brought back Charles II, who discreetly favoured Catholicism, and then his brother James II (1685-88), who was a convinced Catholic — but not a very prudent one, for he failed to prevent the 'Glorious Revolution' which forced him into exile and gave the throne to his daughter and her ultra-protestant husband William of Orange — William III of England. The conversion of Christina and the England of the Stuarts had awakened fresh hopes at Rome, hopes which ended entombed in St Peter's.

25

The Great French Century

The seventeenth century was a great French century, in religious matters also. The ally of the Protestants as far as external affairs were concerned, France in its internal policy moved from the tolerance granted by the edict of Nantes, to strict catholic unity. Despite the shadows cast by Jansenism, French Christianity was wonderfully vital. Yet the proliferation of theological disputes was a sign of religious restlessness and of spiritual instability.

1. In the seventeenth century France took over from Spain as the leading power in Europe, and also as the principal focus of catholic vitality. The wars of religion had ended in a compromise: Henry IV became a Catholic, France continued to be a catholic country and the Huguenots received in the edict of Nantes (1598) a guarantee of toleration. A new period of religious splendour now began. We have already spoken of St Francis de Sales and his work of direction of souls. St Vincent de Paul (1581-1660) promoted missions to the people at large, training priests for this at the seminary of St Lazare (Lazarists) and also did much welfare work, especially through his foundation of the Daughters of Charity. New religious congregations were born, such as that founded by St John Baptist de la Salle for education, and the Cistercian Order was reformed by Abbot Rancé — the start of the Trappists.

2. The French school of spirituality, which reached its peak in this period, was concerned particularly with raising the standard of the diocesan clergy (very much in line with the tridentine decrees). This was the main purpose of the Oratory, founded by Cardinal Bérulle, and of J.J. Olier's Sulpicians, at the seminaries of St Sulpice, a training-ground for teachers for other diocesan seminaries. Christian intellectual life was enriched by really outstanding personalities: for example, Blaise Pascal, an extraordinary thinker and mathematician; the Benedictine, Mabillon, the author of a huge work of historical scholarship, and prelates as famous as Bossuet and Fénelon. Louis XIII's vow (1637) consecrating his kingdom to the Blessed Virgin was a sort of symbol of the catholic golden age in France. It should be pointed out that France's policy of external alliance with the protestant princes did not imply sympathy or favour towards the huguenot minority within the country. In fact, Louis XIV actually put a stop to the earlier toleration and, revoking the edict of Nantes, imposed catholic unity by force.

3. The seventeenth century was a time of theological disputes — an indication of the generally high interest taken in religious questions; but these controversies also suggest a state of latent spiritual instability. One question especially attracted the attention of theologians — the relationship between divine grace and the human will in man's justification. The council of Trent had declared that grace and freedom acted together in the production of meritorious works; but it did not say how this happened. Luis de Molina (1535-1600), a priest, had laid the stress on the role of human freedom in personal salvation (Molinism); but his critics, led by Father Banez, felt that this did not respect God's omnipotence and omnicausality. The dispute got worse, with molinist Jesuits accusing the Banezists of tending towards Calvinism, while Dominican Banezists thought Molinism was semi-Pelagian because it limited the scope of grace. The Holy See stepped in and a special congregation studied the question over nine years but never produced a statement. Paul V (1605-21), not inclining to one side or other, wanted to put an end to the argument and simply prohibited any one on either side from censuring his opponent in any way. This stance was confirmed by Urban VIII in 1625 and 1641, and by Innocent X in 1654.

4. Molinist doctrine and 'probabilist' treatises of moral theology were regarded by some Catholics as fostering a dangerous laxism. One extreme example of this view is to be found in the *Augustinus* of Cornelius Jansen, professor of the University of Louvain and later bishop of Ypres (+ 1638). In this treatise Jansen taught a doctrine on grace which was based on the most rigorous theses formulated by St Augustine in his controversy with Pelagius — where the holy doctor went to the limit in underlining the irresistible strength of the grace God gives the predestined, and man's powerlessness to attain salvation on his own. The consequence of this doctrine was strict moral rigorism and a feeling that 'fear and trembling' should imbue a Christian's relations with God.

5. Jansenism certainly seemed to have something to say, which explains why it was taken up in certain sectors in France where the spiritual life was being actively practised. It was the abbot of Saint-Cyran who introduced Jansenism into France; its centre became the abbey of Port-Royal, a monastery of Cistercian nuns, where the reverend mother Angélique Arnauld introduced a rigorous and severe observance. Angélique's brother, — the 'Great Arnauld' — who came as she did from a distinguished legal family, and a group of solitaries of Port-Royal headed by Pascal, completed the Jansenist group, which was to be the apple of discord among French Catholics for three quarters of a century.

6. It is not possible to detail here all the stages of the Jansenist crisis. It was a long and bitter struggle in which the adversaries of Port-Royal were led by the Jesuits, against whom Pascal wrote his famous *Provinciales*. Papal condemnation of the *Augustinus* (1643) and the Jansenist five propositions (1653) did not put an end to the strife which lasted with some intermission until the start of the eighteenth century. Louis XIV's severity towards the Jansenists (in 1710 he ordered the razing of Port-Royal and in 1713 he obtained from Rome the bull *Unigenitus Dei filius* condemning them) eventually put an end to the overt history of French Jansenism but did not prevent deplorable consequences. In Holland a Jansenist church was formed, which separated from Rome by the schism of Utrecht. But the most serious thing was that the Jansenist crisis, which arose out of a sincere though unbalanced desire for religious authenticity and moral rigour, ended up doing the Church serious harm and preparing the way of the sort of outlook that opened the gates to the irreligious avalanche of the eighteenth century.

7. Contemporaneous with the Jansenist drama was another, although not on the same scale — that of quietism. The creator of quietism was a Spanish priest resident in Rome, Miguel de Molinos (1628-96), who taught a mysticism of total passivity in self-surrender to God. Molinos had many followers in Italy and France; but he and his quietist mysticism ended up being condemned by the Church. This sort of theological dispute, so common in the seventeenth century, even occurred on the missions in connection with the oriental rites controversy. In India, the Jesuit father Nobili, keen to obtain conversions among the Brahmins, thought it made sense to tolerate usages and customs not inseparably linked with pagan religion. In China, the Jesuit missionaries followed a similar policy and tried to adapt Christianity to the ways of Chinese culture. The main concession they made had to do with the name used to designate God, and tolerance in the form of allowing Chinese Catholics to continue to render traditional honours to Confucius and their ancestors. Other missionaries thought this was going much too far and at the end of a long controversy the pope refused to admit the 'oriental rites', despite the disadvantage this would have on the spread of the gospel.

8. No survey of the seventeenth century theological scene would be complete without recalling an episode which has had far more impact on later generations than it did on its contemporaries — the trial of Galileo. As is known, his theories on the immobility of the sun and the rotation and movement of the earth were condemned in 1616 by a commission of theologians as being philosophically absurd and formally heretical, since they seemed to contradict certain passages of the Bible where it speaks of the earth not moving and the sun moving. This condemnation was confirmed when Galileo appeared in person before the Holy Office in 1633. The trial and condemnation of Galileo — deplored by the second Vatican council and by Pope John Paul II — have often been used as an argument to show the incompatibility of religion and science. Undoubtedly the Roman ecclesiastics made a serious mistake in trying to use theological methods to judge a scientific hypothesis, thereby failing to respect the lawful autonomy of science. But it is unreasonable to draw from this episode the conclusion that religion and science are incompatible. To put the facts in their context, it is interesting to note that Galileo defended his theories with a conviction derived from the strength of his genius; but the physical proof of the truth of his theories did not come until centuries later.

26

Royal Absolutism *versus* the Papacy

The governments of the catholic monarchies of the eighteenth century were inclined towards absolutism; they were hostile towards and jealous of the papacy, and tried to control every smallest aspect of church life and make the Church little more than a government ministry. Gallicanism, Josephinism and Febronianism are expressions of one and the same phenomenon of royal interference in the activity of the Church, as one would expect of 'enlightened despotism'.

1. The seventeenth and eighteenth centuries were a period of growth in the political supremacy of the protestant powers in Europe — England, Holland, Sweden, Prussia. In contrast to this, Protestantism on the religious level suffered increasingly from the disintegrating effects of that free examination which formed its birthright — doctrinal instability and more and more divisions. The immutability of dogma began to be used as an argument of apologists in favour of the truth of Catholicism. Bossuet wrote a book on the history of changes in the protestant churches, to prove that they were not the true Church. Some Protestants were also aware of the dangers of such doctrinal fluidity, and the synod of Dordrecht (Holland) in 1618-19 compiled a profession of orthodox faith to be subscribed to by all pastors who wished to stay in the bosom of the reformed church. The fragmentation of the great protestant confessions into sects and groups also proved to be impossible to prevent. Within Protestantism only one great voice was raised in favour not just of unity among the reformed churches but also with the catholic Church, to return to the full unity of Christians — the voice of Leibniz, who for more than ten years kept up a debate with Bossuet, in search of grounds for understanding which would show the way to Christian reconciliation.

2. The absolutism of the Sun King, Louis XIV, opened the way to the 'enlightened despotism' of the Old Régime. An outburst of ecclesiastical nationalism and nit-picking resentment against the Holy See shook the Bourbon kingdoms and others: although they made a point of recognizing Catholicism as the state religion, they tended to see the Church almost as a public service in the sense of a facility the state was responsible for. Official Catholicism, distrust of Rome and state interventionism were the main components of this eighteenth century absolutism in so far as it affected religion.

3. Louis XIV, as we have said, re-established the full catholic unity of France by rescinding the edict of Nantes which previously had guaranteed toleration to his huguenot subjects. But this did not prevent the king from clashing with the Holy See when he tried to extend to all vacant bishoprics and benefices the crown's right of nomination which the 1516 concordat had given it over some of these offices. When Innocent XI protested, the French hierarchy took the side of Louis XIV, and Bossuet, its most distinguished member, composed the famous four 'Organic Articles' (1682) which form the very quintessence of Gallicanism.

4. The 'Organic Articles', which had to be taught in all French seminaries, denied that the pope had the right to release subjects from their oath of fidelity to their sovereign, and formulated a restrictive doctrine on the primatial rights of the papacy. The popes, who must respect the customs of particular churches, are subject to ecumenical councils (exactly what conciliarism tried to do at Constance), and papal decrees on matters of faith are irrefutable only if they have been accepted by the Church. The conflict over nominations was not resolved until 1693, when the order to teach the articles in seminaries was revoked; but the Gallicanist spirit stayed alive in the French clergy until much later.

5. In the eighteenth century, this tendency towards state interventionism in church affairs and hostility to the Roman See spread to all the catholic kingdoms, which were administered either by absolutists or by people inspired by the anti-Christian ideology of the Enlightenment. The favourite target of the anti-Roman offensive was the Society of Jesus, which was regarded as the popes' most powerful weapon. The Jesuit reductions in Paraguay, the business failure of Fr Lavalette in Martinique and the Esquilache riot in Madrid were used in this campaign against the Jesuits, who were expelled from Portugal, Spain and Naples and declared illegal in France. Finally, the society was dissolved by Clement XIV.

6. In the Germanic countries, these absolutist doctrines gave rise to Febronianism, a term derived from Febronius, a pseudonym used by Johann Nikolaus von Hontheim, auxiliary bishop to the elector bishop of Trier. The theses spelt out by Febronius in his book *The Constitution of the Church* once more brought up all the old conciliarist doctrines and gave the council supremacy in a Church where the pope's only function was an administrative one. Additionally, Febronius proposed that churches should be subordinate to princes and that a return should be made to the discipline of a so-called 'primitive church.' Febronius' book was widely read despite being condemned by the pope, and his influence was not dissimilar to the anti-Roman attitude of the three ecclesiastical prince electors of the empire, in the second half of the eighteenth century.

7. This absolutism also took a grip of the Habsburg monarchy, in the form of Josephinism. The Church — according to Emperor Joseph II of Austria — should be more or less a government department, in charge of things to do with worship and the promotion of morality. The whole system of church government must be overseen in detail by the state — from the liturgical calendar to seminary studies; from everything ranging from the government of monasteries to communications with the Roman see. The synod of Pistoia (1786) was an attempt by Bishop Scipione de Ricci to extend Josephinism to the Grand Duchy of Tuscany, whose sovereigns were also Habsburgs.

8. Royal absolutism was undoubtedly the common feature in the ecclesiastical policy of enlightened despotism: this holds true also outside the catholic monarchies we have referred to: thus, Peter the Great — the enlightened despot of the Muscovite empire — in 1723 suppressed the patriarchate of the Russian church, replacing it with a holy synod, closely controlled by the state. By way of summing up, we can conclude that, in the eighteenth century, the states of the Old Régime were still rigorously confessional. The Church enjoyed official protection and still wore the trappings of its traditional privileges. But the church hierarchy in the absolutist monarchies, largely the preserve of the aristocrats, were submissive to the royal power, and their relations with Rome were, at best, limited and distant. On the eve of the era of revolutions, and while irreligion was spreading among the upper classes, Christian life generally seemed to be suffering from anaemia: there was a dearth of great saints, of creativity, of missionary spirit. Even the popes of the eighteenth century, personally quite worthy and respectable, seem, with the exception of Benedict XIV, rather flat and dull. The Christian people in general seemed tired and enervated in these last hours of the Old Régime.

27

The Anti-Christian Enlightenment

From the second half of the seventeenth century many people began to suffer from what has been called 'the crisis of the European conscience.' English deism and French rationalism prepared the ground for the openly anti-Christian work of the philosophers of the 'Enlightenment'. The Encyclopédie *spread these new ideas, which were very well received by the upper classes of society.*

1. *La crise de la conscience européene, 1680–1715*: this was the title of a book by Paul Hazard, which is still perfectly valid today, sixty years after it was published. Hazard concentrated on the thirty-five years of the reign of Louis XIV of France, crucial years which saw the crystallization of ideas and attitudes that created the anti-Christian enlightenment of the eighteenth century. Two hundred years earlier, the protestant crisis had broken the spiritual unity of Europe; but for all that it was a Christian and religious revolt. Now it was Christianity itself and in fact all positive religion that was going to be outlawed. Looking at France, the epicentre of this cataclysm, Hazard summed up in these words the enormous change which occurred between the seventeenth and eighteenth centuries: 'most Frenchmen thought like Bossuet; and, suddenly, they began to think like Voltaire.' We shall now look at how this change came about and what effects it had.

2. Christianity is a revealed religion; it contains truths of a supernatural order which the believer gets access to not by way of direct experience, but through faith. Cartesian rationalism — which played a key part in the shaping of the modern outlook — proclaimed methodical doubt as the basis of human discourse and rejected everything which does not present itself with absolute clarity to human reason. It is true that Descartes (1596-1650) was a Catholic and that he would not have methodical doubt applied to religious faith, for he thought that man has absolute and immediate certainty regarding

God. But, later rationalism — quite logically — gave religion no such special treatment and it ended up denying any value to knowledge based on faith or to revealed truths or the supernatural order.

3. Unbridled rationalism, once it rejects revelation, quickly leads to religious scepticism. Nothing is sure, nothing is certain; everything one formerly believed so firmly is wrong or questionable: this was the conclusion arrived at by Pierre Bayle in his *Historical and Critical Dictionary*. A hedonistic current of thought, led by Saint-Évremond, drew the same conclusion as his predecessors in the times of Isaiah and St Paul: 'let us eat and drink, for tomorrow we die' (Is 22:13; 1 Cor 15:32). The libertines adopted an attitude of evident distaste for religion: they were epicureans; this life and its pleasures was all that mattered. They were as far away from Christianity as it was possible to be.

4. Divine revelation has been transmitted through the valid channel of sacred scripture. Spinoza's radical critique of the Bible used the demolition of certain traditional interpretations (such as that about the age of the world) to put a question-mark over the historical value of all the revealed books. He went further: he even rejected miracles and the supernatural order, putting them on the same plane as legends and superstition. Thus, the replacing of revealed religion with a merely natural religion was that deism aimed at; it originated in England and spread to France and Germany. Unlike atheism, deism did not deny God existed, but it pushed him away into the background. The God of the deists was something invented by reason; often he was pantheistic; there was no such thing as revelation. Deism gave rise to Freemasonry, whose first lodges were founded in Britain in the early eighteenth century; this was a secret society, which rejected all positive religion — especially Christianity — and encouraged brotherhood and philantrophy among its members. Freemasonry was condemned by Clement XII in 1738 and had an undoubted influence on the development of the enlightenment.

5. The year 1715 — the year Louis XIV died — saw the opening of the floodgates of irreligion. In the decades that followed, the *philosophes* literally imposed themselves on the cultural life of France and elsewhere. They were in fact a kind of sect, in which Voltaire performed the role of high priest. Voltaire (1694-1778) was not an original thinker; he drew most of his ideas from the English deists or from Bayle and Spinoza. Nor was he very deep: but he was a brilliant purveyor of ideas, thanks to the clarity of his style and to his skill as a satirist. Hatred of positive religion and especially of Christianity was an obsession with Voltaire; for him the catholic Church was infamous; it must be trodden into the ground. Voltaire's great ambition was to eliminate the Christian religion. 'Jesus Christ', he went so far as to write, 'needed twelve Apostles to spread the gospel; I am going to show that one is enough to destroy it'.

6. The entire core philosophy of the enlightenment was also anti-Christian in its rejection of all dogmatic truth; dogma it regarded *a priori* as an expression of intolerance and fanaticism. Orthodoxy, for the enlightenment, was something fit only for ridicule; it was an expression of the intellectual limitations of retarded minds and enemies of progress. The enlightened, the 'brave spirits', prided themselves on their free-thinking and in the political sphere they advocated indiscriminate toleration of all confessions. The American revolution, therefore, had a great impact on France, and the solution adopted by the United States (where the constitution proclaimed separation of Church and state, and freedom of worship) seemed to the enlightened to be an example which all Europe should imitate. However, it should be pointed out that the motivations behind tolerance were not at all the same in America as in the ideology of the *philosophes*. American tolerance was based on the pluralism of American society, where there was a whole constellation of religious creeds and confessions. The toleration the *philosophes* wanted to install in countries where the whole ethos was catholic was based on the ideological principle of dogmatic relativism.

7. In the second half of the eighteenth century, catholic unity was still very much a fact over very broad sectors of society in the Latin countries of Europe. Spain and Italy were not greatly influenced by the enlightenment. But in France it was different: there the new philosophy flourished among the aristocracy and upper bourgeoisie, affecting even the urban middle class. A very effective tool to popularize this enlightenment ideology was the *Encyclopédie;*, the first work of its kind, planned by Diderot and D'Alembert and written in 1751-72 by a team of editors who came to be called the encyclopaedists. The *Encyclopédie* adopted an intellectually hostile attitude to Christianity, whose 'incompatibility' with the experimental sciences or the demands of reason it sought to refer to at every opportunity. The naturalistic rationalism of Jean Jacques Rousseau (1712-78) — whose deism was clear from his *Profession of Faith of the Savoyard Vicar* — had a big influence on the religious ideology of the *Encyclopédie*.

8. In protestant Germany, the enlightenment took its own form as the *Aufklärung*. It outlined a 'reasonable' Christianity, without dogmas or miracles, something similar to the later liberal Protestantism. But Immanuel Kant (1724-1804), the leading German thinker of the period, exposed a dilemma by considering religion from the distinct points of view of pure and practical reason. On the speculative level Kant tried to refute the reason-based arguments for the existence of God: 'I have therefore found it necessary,' he wrote, 'to deny knowledge in order to make room for faith.' The practical reason, on the other hand, allows man to reach absolute certainty of God's existence and of the immortality of the soul. Kant had a great influence on nineteenth century European thought.

9. In conclusion, it can be said that rationalism, religious naturalism (no mystery, no supernatural order), negative criticism of positive religions and especially of Christianity, and a general attitude of intellectual rebellion were what shaped the 'enlightened' outlook of the eighteenth century. Even in France, this philosophical spirit was limited to a small minority — but they were influential people; the people at large kept to their religious faith and practice. But it was this minority which was going to decide which intellectual banner would fly over the new era starting with the outbreak of the French revolution.

From Revolution to Restoration

The revolutionary era which started in 1789 shook the political and religious foundations of Europe. The French revolution, at its climax, tried to blot out every trace of Christianity from the life of society. Two popes were imprisoned by the revolutionary governments. Napoleon, who restored the Church in France, also assumed the inheritance of Gallicanism. The restoration of the Bourbons tried to elect a return of the Old Régime. Many Catholics, after their terrible experience during the revolution, proposed a new 'alliance between throne and altar.'

1. During the quarter century from 1789 to 1815 France occupied the centre of the world stage. This period, which ran from the opening of the states general to the fall of the Napoleonic empire, was also of transcendental importance for the destinies of Christianity and the Church. We shall look at the main lines of this period from the Christian point of view, which is what interests us.

2. It is well known — though it sounds like a paradox — that the French revolution began with a solemn procession, presided over by King Louis XVI, with the representatives of the three estates, holding candles, devoutly following the blessed sacrament. This happened on 4 May 1789, at the opening of the states general; but within a few weeks the whole scene had changed and the revolutionary process advanced at breakneck speed, in both the political and religious sphere. On 4 August 1789, in a memorable 'patriotic session' of the national assembly, the clergy and the nobility renounced their traditional privileges. On 10 October, on the proposal of Talleyrand, then bishop of Autun, the constituent assembly decreed the secularization of all church property — which soon found its way into private hands and formed the financial base of the new French bourgeoisie.

3. From 1790, the revolutionary process adopted an ever more aggressive attitude towards the Church. On 13 February 1790 a decision was taken to suppress monastic vows, and on 12 July 1790 the assembly approved the 'civil constitution of the clergy', which totally undermined the Church's administrative system. A Gallican church arose, already independent of papal authority, episcopalian and presbyterian in structure, with the bishops and clergy being elected by the people and Rome simply being notified of appointments. The assembly required priests to swear fidelity to the political constitution, within which was included this 'constitution of the clergy.' Pope Pius VI forbade them to do so and excommunicated those priests who disobeyed (13 March 1791). A schism was thus created between the 'juring' and the 'non-juring' priests, the latter becoming suspect in the eyes of the law. The legislative assembly which followed on the constituent assembly, decreed on 27 May 1792 the deportation of the non-juring priests; in September the convention took over from the legislative assembly and started to execute priests. The monarchy was abolished, a republic was declared and Louis XVI was executed on 21 January 1793.

4. The years 1793-4 were the most tragic of the revolutionary period. Under the Terror, anti-catholic persecution reached its climax. Thousands of victims died on the scaffold and an effort was made to blot out every trace of Christianity from the life of society. Even the calendar was replaced with a republican calendar. The enthronement of the Goddess of Reason in the cathedral of Notre Dame (10 November 1793) and the institution by Robespierre of the cult of the Supreme Being were other episodes in this dechristianization attempt, which also took the form of iconoclasm — the mark of which can be seen in old French cathedrals and churches even today. The following years were marked by lulls and then renewed persecution. One of the worst points was under the Jacobin directory (1795-9), when the French occupied Rome and proclaimed the Roman republic. Pope Pius VI, old and infirm, was deported to Siena, Florence and finally France. On 29 August 1799 in the fortress of Valence-sur-Rhône he died, at the age of eighty-one. Some fanatical revolutionaries boasted that the last pope had died.

5. On 9 November of the same year, the *coup d'état* of 18 Brumaire brought Napoleon Bonaparte to the position of first consul; four months later — 14 March 1800 — the conclave met in Venice and elected Cardinal Chiaramonti as Pope Pius VII: two great personalities thus appeared on the scene of history. Napoleon, pragmatic and realistic, was conscious of how deeply rooted the Christian religion was among the French people, despite what happened during the revolution. Pius VII, for his part, ardently wanted to see the life of the Church return to normal in France. A concordat was devised between the papacy and the republic (which soon would become an empire); it was signed on 15 July 1801 and one of its results was the creation of a new episcopacy, both 'constitutional' bishops and 'legitimate' bishops (*emigrés*) resigning. Unilaterally and without consulting the Holy See, Napoleon promulgated, along with the text of the concordat, seventy-seven Organic Articles which contained the spirit and sometimes even the letter of the old Gallican Articles imposed by Louis XIV in 1682.

6. The concordat had certainly some favourable results for the Church: it allowed Christian life in France to be rebuilt (this was helped also by a renewal of religious feeling that came with early romanticism, in reaction against the dry rationalism of the enlightenment). Chateaubriand's *Le Génie du Christianisme* faithfully reflects this kind of feeling. The concordat made it possible to open seminaries (maintained with state funds) and therefore the training of a new clergy, but Napoleon was very restrictive with regard to religious orders. It should, however, be pointed out that during the Napoleonic period a body of opinion grew up in France which was clearly opposed to Christianity and to the Church; it was made up of people with different backgrounds — people who owned confiscated church property, public officials, professional soldiers, intellectuals of the Institute of France and workers of the new urban proletariat which was just beginning to emerge. These sectors of opinion would be opposed to the Church right through the nineteenth century.

7. The time soon arrived when Napoleon tried to use the Church and the papacy itself to promote his own political interests; but he met serene but resolute resistance from the popes. The clash with the pope arose when the emperor wanted him to join in the continental blockade against England, decreed in November 1806. Napoleon reacted violently to the pope's refusal: he annexed the papal states and declared Rome the second capital of the empire. Pius VII was imprisoned and deported to Savona (6 July 1809) and, when he refused to confirm the decrees of a pseudo-council held in Paris (1811), Napoleon ordered his transfer to France where he assigned him the palace of Fontainebleau as his residence (June 1812). In 1814 Pius was set free and on 7 June 1815 he returned definitively to Rome. Eleven days later — on 18 June 1815 — a new name became part of world history — Waterloo.

8. The restoration tried to roll back the map of Europe as if nothing had happened in the previous twenty-five years. Christianity and the Church had been severely tested and bore the marks of wounds inflicted by the revolution. Is it surprising that the Church regarded the end of the revolutionary period like the end of a nightmare, and saluted the return of the 'good old times' as a liberation? The 'alliance of throne and altar', created in the belief that by each supporting the other both would be secure, was the ideal many Catholics dreamed of at this time. But, for good or ill, the restoration did not last long, and after unsuccessful attempts in 1820 to set it aside in Spain, Portugal, Naples and Piedmont, from 1830 onwards the dynamism of the bourgeoisie set the revolutionary process in motion again.

29

Catholicism and Liberalism

The restoration failed. The nineteenth century was the century of liberalism, the ideology of the bourgeois revolution. Could an understanding be reached between Catholicism and liberalism? Would it suit the Church simply to be free, without the protection of the state or recognition of the Church's traditional privileges? Should truth and error have equal rights in public life? These and other questions were answered in different ways by Catholics in this period, which also witnessed the rise of nationalism, which directly threatened the papal states.

1. The restoration ended in failure and the nineteenth century passed into history as the century of liberalism. The revolution of 1830 put an end to the Old Régime in France; in Spain it disappeared after the death of Ferdinand VII, in the reign of Isabella II. The revolution of 1848 was an earthquake which affected most of Europe and led eventually to important social and political changes. The victory of liberalism was felt in all aspects of life. Here we will look at its effects on Christianity and the Church.

2. Liberalism had a political and an economic doctrine; but it was based on an ideology closely connected with the 'enlightened' thought of the eighteenth century. At the basis of this liberal theology is an anthropocentric view of the world and of existence. For liberalism, men are not only free and equal: they are autonomous, that is to say, they are bound by no law given by God: society does not recognize God's law as the supreme norm. Freedom of conscience and of thought, of association and of the press, are people's inalienable rights; and in reply to the traditional Christian teaching that power derives from God, for liberalism it comes from the people; the people are the only source of legitimate government. Liberal doctrine made no distinction between the true religion (Christianity) and other religions. Religion, for liberalism, is a private matter, to do with the intimacy of conscience, and the Church, separate from the state ('a free Church in a free state') is something on the fringe of public life and is subject to state law, as is every other association.

3. Liberal ideology certainly contained elements of genuine Christian provenance, but mixed in with others of very different origin which favoured the secularization of social life, religious naturalism and, ultimately, atheism or indifference. It is easy to understand why many Christians rejected such an ideology out of hand and, having learned their lessons in their recent experience with the revolutions, were inclined to favour traditionalist positions, which called for respect for the rights of God and of the Church in the life of society. These anti-liberal Catholics were sympathetic towards the counter-revolutionary governments which still existed in Europe — governments which to some degree, at least, kept the Old Régime going and recognized the Church as having a position of privilege in society.

4. Around the year 1830 a group of liberal Catholics gathered around the *L'Avenir*, a journal edited by Félicité de Lamennais. In opposition to the tradionalist position which most Catholics held to, these favoured a reconciliation, not so much theoretical as practical, of the Church with liberalism; they were convinced that liberalism was there to stay and that the Church could not fulfil its specific mission without being in harmony with it. 'God and liberty' was the motto of liberal Catholicism — meaning that acceptance and defence of liberty for all and in all its forms were the best credentials for ensuring that modern society would show respect for God's authority and for the Church's rights.

5. Initially 'liberal Catholics' were 'ultramontanes', and in France rejected Gallicanism; they looked 'beyond the mountains', towards Rome, and showed reverence to the papacy, the cornerstone of the universal Church. But Rome's reply did not meet with their expectations. Gregory XVI's encyclical *Mirari vos* (15 August 1832) condemned a number of basic points of the programme of the *L'Avenir* group — equality of treatment for all beliefs which, the pope said, led to indifferentism; complete separation between Church and state; freedom of conscience; unlimited freedom of opinion and of the press. This papal rebuff was followed immediately by Lamennais' defection; he left the priesthood and the Church. But his principal colleagues reacted otherwise: they stayed faithful to the Church; Lacordaire restored the Dominican Order in France; others, like Montalembert and Falloux, professed a less radical liberalism and campaigned in favour of freedom of education from state control.

6. Catholic Christianity and liberalism met also in another area. The explosion of nationalism, much favoured by liberal policies, led to the emancipation of catholic populations which had been under the dominion of rulers of a different confession. The liberals applauded the repeated uprisings of catholic Poland against oppression by czarist Russia. The revolution of 1830 led to an alliance between Belgian Catholics and liberals, who managed to withdraw Belgium from the control of the Calvinist monarchy of Holland and gave the new kingdom a liberal constitution. Daniel O'Connell, in the name of civil and religious liberty, obtained substantial emancipation for the Irish people, and in Britain liberal reforms improved the position of Catholics by getting rid of many old laws which discriminated on grounds of religion. All these helpful results of liberal nationalist movements should not make us forget the dangers those same movements implied in one area very particularly connected with the Apostolic See — the Italian peninsula, where the *Risorgimento* was all the rage; the route of this movement to national unity lay through the disappearance of the papal states and the turning of papal Rome into the capital of the kingdom of Savoy.

7. This survey of the encounter between Christianity and liberalism would be incomplete if it does not refer to anti-religious intellectual attitudes at the root of attacks against the Christian view of man and the world: these attitudes developed in virulence in the nineteenth century. The positivism of Auguste Comte argued that, in the new era of human history, now that the theological and metaphysical stages had been superseded, man was interested mainly in phenomena, in the 'how' of things and events and not in the barren 'whys' of other ages. Positivism led to scientism — really religion without any supernatural dimension — which must supplant Christianity, exposing every mystery, 'explaining' reality and bringing happiness and unlimited progress to mankind. Positivism and the idealism of the great German philosopher Hegel were at the basis of Feuerbach's materialism, which is very close to Marxism.

8. All these doctrines acted as a base for a generalized offensive against Christianity, in the field of science, particularly the natural sciences. But even the sacred sciences became the cockpit of this anti-Christian struggle. The critique of the historicity of sacred scripture (emptying it of supernatural content) led Strauss to deny that Christ ever existed and moved Ernest Renan (who was less daring but more subtle) to write a famous *Life of Jesus*, of a Jesus who is no longer God, though he is the noblest of the sons of men. It is clear that the intellectual and political climate of Pius IX's time was fraught with threats, sometimes provoking the Church to interfere — with unhappy results — in temporal affairs. But the renewed Christian vitality which can also be noticed in this period is a good indication that all times are God's times, in spite of men and in spite of how things look on the surface.

30

The Era of Pius IX

The long pontificate of Pius IX covered a whole era. Pius IX was a pope much loved and respected by Catholics; even the misfortunes which befell him helped strengthen these feelings towards him. This was a period in Christian history which saw a great deal of renewal in things to do with the internal life of the Church. It also saw the holding of the first Vatican council and the loss of the papal states.

1. The pontificate of Pius IX lasted thirty-two years — from 1846 to 1878, the longest in the history of the papacy. The story is told that, during the ceremony of his coronation, when the cardinal protodeacon said the traditional words, 'Holy Father, you will not attain the days of Peter', Pius IX replied brightly, 'That is not a matter of faith.' And as it turned out Pius IX's papacy lasted much longer than St Peter's; so long in fact that one can speak of the era of Pius IX as a well-defined chapter in Christian history. It is a chapter which also takes in the transition from the last days of the Old Régime to the consolidation of the liberal world.

2. 'We had foreseen everything, except a liberal pope'. This was how Prince Metternich, chancellor of the Austro-Hungarian empire and creator of the Holy Alliance, greeted the election of Pius IX. But the 'liberalism' of Pius IX was just one more indication of how ambiguous the word 'liberal' is. The new pope was indeed a liberal man — but in the sense of someone who practises the virtue of liberality, not in that he was a follower of the doctrines of liberalism. Pius IX was a cordial, generous, magnanimous person who did not hesitate to introduce a series of progressive reforms in the papal states immediately he was elected — political amnesty, improvements in public administration, and even a constitution and a government with a civil prime minister. These reforms made the pope enormously popular. He was everywhere acclaimed and the neo-Guelphs, such as Gioberti or D'Azeglio (Catholic nationalist liberals), even thought under his aegis to achieve that Italian unity sought by the *Risorgimento*.

3. But as might have been foreseen, it soon became clear that this was a mistake. Pius IX — an Italian at heart — refused to head up a national league to fight a 'holy war' against the Austrians who controlled the north of the peninsula. As quickly as he had acquired it, the pope lost his popularity and soon became the subject of abuse. In November 1848, Pellegrino Rossi, the prime minister of the papal states, was stabbed to death at the door of parliament by the zealots of Young Italy. In February 1849 Mazzini proclaimed the Roman republic and the pope had to flee in disguise to Gaeta, a military stronghold in the neighbouring kingdom of Naples. When he returned to Rome, in April 1850, under the protection of French troops, he carried deep impressions of his bitter experiences. From then on, he saw liberalism as a movement which he had a sacred duty to oppose, because the ideal it pursued was not Christian — and because in Italy it was trying to wrest the papal states from the Holy See.

4. The defence of the temporal power of the popes lasted twenty years — from 1850 to 1870. Bit by bit pieces of the papal states fell to the Piedmontese kingdom, soon to be the kingdom of Italy. In 1870, the start of the Franco-Prussian War meant that the French garrison at Rome had to be withdrawn; the city was then taken by the soldiers of Victor Emmanuel II, who made it the capital of the new Italy. Meanwhile, the pope withdrew into the Vatican, as a voluntary prisoner, rejecting the Law of Guarantees which he was offered, and the 'Roman question' began, which took sixty years to solve.

5. Perhaps it is difficult for many people nowadays, in view of the present position of the pope in the world, to understand why Pius IX put so much effort into trying to hold on to his temporal power. But history does not yield up the truth unless it is seen through the eyes of the people who actually made it. Pius IX defended his rights to the very end because these rights were a precious legacy he had received from his predecessors in the papacy. And, what was more, because those states, which had existed for over one thousand years, were regarded at the time as an essential guarantee of the independence of the popes in the government of the universal Church.

6. The Church's position on the principles of liberalism was spelt out by Pius IX in his encyclical *Quanta cura* (8 December 1864). This encyclical carried, as an appendix, a 'syllabus', a list of eighty propositions summing up 'modern errors', each of which was the subject of an express condemnation. The document did not contain anything substantially new, for all the errors had been condemned in earlier texts of the magisterium. What was new was the form and the uncompromising accent these propositions seemed to contain now that they were taken and put side by side, now that it was all being spelt out in one document. The 'syllabus' anathematized the absolute autonomy of reason, religious naturalism, indifferentism, materialism, attacks on the family, the defence of divorce, etc. The last proposition in the document, which rejected what some people claimed was the pope's duty to come to terms with progress and 'modern civilization', made liberal critics really tear their garments — and went down very well with traditionalist Catholics.

7. Leaving aside the political upheavals of the time, Pius IX's pontificate was one of great vitality in the life of the Church. The old religious orders — like the Benedictines of Dom Guéranger; the Dominicans, invigorated by Lacordaire, and the Jesuits, restored by Pius VII — grew and spread quite considerably; and new religious congregations arose, one of the more important of which was the Salesians, of Don Bosco. The clergy generally improved — more vocations and a higher level of observance (also to be seen in a return to a generalized use of ecclesiastical dress). For these secular clergy, the Curé d'Ars, St Jean Marie Vianney, was an example of heroic sanctity in the person of a humble country parish priest. The ordinary faithful, similarly, became actively involved in new apostolic and social welfare initiatives, among the most outstanding of which were the Conferences of St Vincent de Paul, created by Fréderic Ozanam.

8. At the very same time as the waves of anti-religion were lashing the Church, a powerful spiritual impulse was animating nineteenth-century Christianity. In the heart of Anglicanism it produced the Oxford movement, which led the finest spirits, eagerly searching for Christian authenticity, to their genuine roots, that is, to the gates of the Church. Some went no further; but others took the decisive step and crossed the threshold of the Church: John Henry Newman was received into the Church (1845), and both he and his fellow Anglican Manning — later on in their lives — were made cardinals. Two other factors which point up the deep religious dimension of Pius IX's pontificate are the definition of the dogma of the immaculate conception (8 December 1854), followed four years later by appearances of the Blessed Virgin at Lourdes, and the holding of the first Vatican council (1869-70). This council, despite its short

life (due to political events), approved two very important resolutions: the dogma of papal infallibility, and the constitution *Dei Filius*, which formulated the teaching of the Church on the central religious question of the nineteenth century — the problem of the relationship between faith and reason.

9. When it comes to assessing the era of Pius IX, an observer who focusses only on temporal aspects and on political events must surely decide that the Church came out losing: the pope lost the papal states, the catholic cantons of Switzerland lost out to the Protestants in the Sonderbund war (1847) and the last years of Pius IX were overshadowed by anti-clerical violence and the attacks of Bismarck's *Kulturkampf* against the German Catholics. Yet, if one looks at it with supernatural outlook, Pius IX's reign was a very positive one for Christianity and the Church, and it opened the way to the modern papacy. A very important development was the entirely new phenomenon of pope and people of God coming together — something made possible by the development of communications (railways, steamships) which made it much easier for Catholics to make the journey to Rome. Thanks to this and to the speed of communication by telegraph, the pope ceased to be someone remote and distant: he became accessible, and even his misfortunes endeared him to the faithful. It has been said, with good reason, that Pius IX was the first 'loved' pope in modern history. For the first time Catholics looked to and loved the pope as a father, and his lithograph presided, like a family portrait, over catholic homes around the world.

31

Christianity in a New Kind of Society

The nineteenth century also witnessed big changes in society. The rise of capitalism, the industrial revolution and the creation of the urban proletariat created a 'social problem', which had never before existed. Anti-Christian ideologies, like Marxism and anarchism, proposed new models for society and exercised a strong influence on workers' movements. Pope Leo XIII proposed a Christian programme for the new world of work.

1. Nineteenth-century liberalism had a political ideology and an economic doctrine. But it had no social conscience, no sense of social responsibility: yet the 'social question' was an obvious fact and one of the new phenomena of the period. The industial revolution had led to the creation of a new working class — a proletariat — concentrated in industrial areas of large cities. In the heyday of capitalism the conditions of the working class were deplorable: long working hours, low wages, child labour, bad living conditions were some of the many injustices which workers suffered.

2. Naturally, various different attempts were made to deal with the injustices of the social question. Anarchism, one of whose main authors was the Russian Mikhail Bakunin, proposed it be solved by violence — putting an end to the state and unjust social structures. Various socialist systems, thought up by Saint-Simon, Fourier, Proudhon and others, were soon eclipsed by the 'scientific' socialism of Karl Marx — Marxism —, whose ideological content we cannot discuss here. From the Christian point of view (which is what concerns us), we must remember that Marxism, based on historical materialism and the dialectic of the class struggle, showed itself to be opposed to all religions which it considered to be a cause of alienation ('the opium of the people'), and Marxism was particularly hostile towards the catholic religion. Atheism or, rather, Marxist anti-theism has done much to dechristianize the working classes — and even society as a whole — in many countries of the world.

3. The proletariat, living on the outskirts of the larger cities, often included a high proportion of immigrants from rural areas, who had drifted from the farms to work in the new industries. This meant that they left the towns and villages where their roots were and became part of the depersonalized mass of the new working class. This often had negative effects from the religious point of view. For centuries the rural population and the artizans in the cities had been part of the Church's pastoral structures and the traditions of Christian society had imbued their lives. But in the industrial suburbs where the new proletariat was crowded on top of itself, things were quite different. The industrial workers felt the impact of Marxist and anarchist doctrines which used them as the vanguard of the revolutionary struggle and in some countries filled them with hostility towards the Church and Christianity.

4. Even from early on in the nineteenth century, some Catholics, concerned about the social question, made various efforts to assuage its effects through charitable and welfare activities. But, in general, Christians were slow to take the problem to heart. It was in some non-Latin countries, less affected by anti-clericalism, that we find the Church getting actively involved in the world of work. Thus, in the United States and in Britain, where there were large numbers of Catholics in the working-class population, the roots of trade unionism were not Marxist but Christian, if anything. It is significant, for example, that Cardinal Manning helped resolve the London dock strike of 1889. In 1864, Von Ketteler, the bishop of Mainz, was already pressing the urgent need 'to solve the great problem of our time, the social question.'

5. A large amount of documentation on the social question was assembled by the first Vatican council but the abrupt end of the council prevented it from dealing with this matter. Some years later Pope Leo XIII did tackle it, in his encyclical *Rerum novarum*. The pope was well aware of the gravity of the problem and of the need for effective action by Christians. Trade unions were the best way of going about the protection of workers' rights. In 1889, Leo had written to Cardinal Manning: 'Oppose socialist associations with popular Christian ones . . . Leave the sacristies, go out to the people'. Two years later (15 May 1891) he published his famous encyclical, which rejected on principle the dialectic of class struggle and asked owners and workers to work together in harmony to develop a new society. The pope proclaimed the social responsibility attaching to property, and the just wage, and appealed to the state to stop being a mere spectator (that was the state's role, as preached by liberalism) and to take control of economic relationships, without going as far as the socialist planned economy. *Rerum novarum* concluded by calling for the creation of Christian-inspired trade unions. Leo XIII's pontificate marks the beginning of social Catholicism, within which it would soon be possible to identify a corporativist tendency and a (more politicized) progressive democratic tendency.

6. Leo XIII held to Pius IX's *non expedit* policy which forbade Italian Catholics to have any involvement in political life. But in other countries the pope tried to shed defensive positions and pursue an intelligent diplomatic policy — which increased the Holy See's prestige and meant that many old *casus belli* became forgotten. Thus in Germany, for example, the empire called off its *Kulturkampf* and even submitted to the Holy See's arbitration in its dispute with Spain over the Caroline and Marshall Islands. But it was in French papal relations that Leo's directive led to important changes in policy.

7. After the fall of the second empire, an attempt to restore the Bourbons failed; gradually, the Third Republic stabilized, under the control of a republican party which dominated political life from 1877 onwards. French republicanism was deeply hostile to the Church: 'Clericalism, that is the enemy' was Gambetta's war-cry. French republicans, very influenced by the ideology of the *Education League,* had as prime objectives the fight against religious congregations and the establishment of the 'lay' schools (which came in 1882) by Jules Ferry, minister for public education, who on some occasion called his ministry 'the ministry of souls'. The French Catholics were almost all of them monarchists, and this republican sectarianism only served to increase their opposition to a régime which they regarded as an enemy of the Church. Leo XIII stepped in to try to solve this problem threatening religious life in France.

8. Leo first encouraged Catholics to take part in public life. In his encyclical *Immortale Dei* (1 November 1885) he had shown the Church's readiness to be on good terms with any system of government, including republican democratic government. Applying these directives, Leo invited French Catholics to cooperate with the Republic: this was the policy of *ralliement,* announced in a famous toast given by Cardinal Lavigerie in Algeria in 1890. In Spain, also, the integration of Pidal's Catholic Union into the political system there was at one with what Leo XIII was saying about Catholics taking part in political life.

9. The beginning of the twentieth century coincided with the end of Leo XIII's pontificate, which had lasted so long that it too could be considered as another whole chapter in church history. The elderly pope had gained the respect of the whole world, even though in some quarters, such as France, his efforts at conciliation obtained little response. His encyclicals constituted an important body of church teaching; and his solemn restoration of Thomistic philosophy had a particularly valuable effect of the renewal of Christian thought. But the presence of Catholics in politico-social life also had its risks; and inside the Church itself a new doctrinal crisis was incubating.

32

St Pius X and the Modernist Crisis

Arising by a whole series of factors — including irreligious philosophies, nineteenth-century scientism and liberal Protestantism — Modernism began to take shape in the Church. Some people expected Modernism to reconcile Catholicism and the modern mind and to bridge the so-called gap between faith and science; but in practice Modernism emptied the catholic faith of its supernatural content. Pius X decisively closed the door on Modernism. He was a courageous pope who concerned himself above all with 'the interests of God' and energetically fostered Christian piety.

1. The first years of the twentieth century, up to the start of the first world war, will always be remembered as a brilliant and happy period in European history, which was brought to an end by the most useless and absurd of wars. But from the Christian point of view it was not at all without its problems — some due to the hostility of enemies outside; others originating within the Church itself, a Church ruled by the last pope to merit canonization, St Pius X (1903-14).

2. During those years, anticlericalism was really making itself felt, especially in the Latin countries of Europe — all of which had Catholic majority populations. Portugal, after its proclamation of a republic (1910), expelled religious from the country, separated the Church from the state and confiscated the Church's property. But France was the scene of the most violent attack on the Church.

3. Radical French governments flaunted their laicism, causing a confrontation with Pius X (aided by his faithful secretary of state Merry del Val). France broke off relations with the Holy See and abrogated its concordat (1905); religious lost the right to teach and many were expelled from the country. Church property was also confiscated which meant that the French church, for the second time in a century, was despoiled of its patrimony and deprived of the state help it had been receiving, since Napoleon's time, in compensation for the previous confiscation. From now on priests and churches were dependent on contribution from church members and the Church's title to ownership of church buildings was no stronger than the fact it occupied them.

4. But difficulties of this kind, which the Church and Catholics encountered in a number of European countries in the early years of the twentieth century were nothing in comparison with the doctrinal problems which arose inside the Church itself. Already, at the end of the nineteenth century, Leo XIII had denounced 'Americanism', which proposed that, in the light of Catholicism's experience in the United States, the Church in Europe, to be more effective, should adapt itself to the new times and give greater importance to the natural virtues and the active life. But the great doctrinal crisis which hit the Church — it was probably *the* event of the Pius X period — was the modernist crisis.

5. Modernism in its origins may have stemmed from the desire of some Catholics to prevent what they saw as the Church's backwardness in the area of historical studies, philosophy and biblical exegesis. Modernism, which was much influenced by liberal Protestantism, tried to rationalize the Christian faith, in order to make it acceptable to the modern mind, freeing it of its deadweight of dogma and even of all supernatural content. The modernists did not try to leave the Church; they wanted to reform it from within, and the positions they took up contained a deliberate ambiguity — in keeping with Tyrrell's saying that Christ had not left men a doctrine but a spirit. Modernism's philosophy was immanentism, which erected 'religious consciousness' as the supreme norm of Christian life. The modernists even designed their own model of a saint, which Fogazzaro used as the hero of his novel *The Saint*.

6. Biblical exegesis, the favourite ground of the modernists, was cultivated by Alfred Loisy, the most outstanding figure in the movement. As if he were dealing with mere historical texts, Loisy applied to the sacred books the rules of rationalist criticism, not taking account of their being inspired books and not listening to the Church's teaching on interpretation of the Bible, repeated by Leo XIII in his encyclical *Providentissimus Deus*. Among the conclusions Loisy arrived at was that the kingdom which is constantly referred to in the gospel was in Christ's mind a purely eschatological one and that the Church was an unforeseen consequence of the fact that the end of the times, which Jesus mistakenly thought imminent, failed to materialize. Therefore, Jesus Christ was not God nor was his resurrection an historical fact: it was the product of the enthusiasm of the first Christian community.

7. Modernist doctrines were never presented as an organic whole. Indeed it was not until the encyclical *Pascendi* (which defined Modernism as 'the crossroads of all heresies') that any attempt was made to present it systematically. As far as its spread is concerned, the modernist movement had a considerable following in certain ecclesiastical and intellectual circles in France, Italy and Britain. Pius X closed the door on Modernism. His decree *Lamentabili* and encyclical *Pascendi* (1907) denounced and condemned these doctrines. Teachers in ecclesiastical institutions and many other clerics were required to take an 'anti-modernist' oath — and this certainly had some effect. So, the modernist crisis was contained by the pope's decisive action. That is not to say that Modernism was overpowered; for it appeared again as a very vigorous growth in the middle of the century.

8. St Pius X also had to deal with some problems arising out of Catholics' involvement in public life. He dissolved the 'Opera dei Congressi,' then very linked with Romolo Murri, on the grounds of its over-involvement in temporal affairs, and put a stop to the activities of the 'democratic priests' in France, where he also condemned Marc Sagnier's *Sillon* movement. But this did not mean that the Church did not still encourage Catholics to engage in politics — as can be seen from the fact that in Italy the *non expedit* was virtually lifted when Catholics were allowed to vote in elections from 1913 forward.

9. The pre-war world received, above all, great spiritual benefit from Pius X's pontificate. The interests of God was the supreme criterion that guided his action in all spheres. It led him to be courageous in his relationships with France and his struggle with Modernism — though some people felt he was not humanly prudent enough. His concern for the holiness of priests, the issuing of a new catechism, the granting of holy communion to children once they had reached the age of reason: these were other signs of his pastoral zeal. It was a zeal which led him to try to improve the life of the Church by reforming its canon law. Under Pius X, the Church adopted the modern practice of codification of law, and it was on his authority that Cardinal Gasparri began the work which was completed by Benedict XV's promulgation of the first Code of Canon Law (1917).

33

The Age of Totalitarianism

The treaty of Versailles brought the world, not peace, but twenty inter-war years. Totalitarianism of different kinds sought to subject the person to the all-embracing will of the state. In Christian countries — like Russia, Mexico and Spain — religious persecution took on very violent forms. Pius XI encouraged Catholic Action as a way of involving the laity in the hierarchical apostolate of the Church. The great expansion of the missions and the solution of the Roman question were two happy events of great importance.

1. The first world war started on 4 August 1914. Two weeks later Pope Pius X died (20 August) — a death symbolic of the millions of men who were to die during the four years of the war. The new pope, Benedict XV (3 September 1914-22 January 1922) could do little more during those years than try to conciliate the belligerent parties. The fighting came to an end in November 1918, thanks to Allied victory over the central empires. The Holy See was excluded from the conference table at Versailles. A century earlier, when Europe was being sorted out after the Napoleonic wars, the Holy See, which still had the papal states, had been present at the Congress of Vienna.

2. The treaty of Versailles did not bring peace: it simply arranged a truce which lasted twenty years. Ignorance of European affairs on the part of the US President, Woodrow Wilson, and France's ancestral resentment of the Habsburgs (now conbined, in Clemenceau, with his personal anti-Catholicism) led, in my view, to the grave political mistake of dismembering the Austro-Hungarian empire. Thus, while allowing northern Germany to survive, centred on protestant Prussia, catholic Germany was dismantled — the Danubian state, the European centre of gravity comprising Germans, Magyars and Slavs. A catholic nation, Poland, was reborn out of its ashes, while another catholic people, Ireland, also achieved a substantial degree of independence at around this time. But the most important event of all, destined to condition the whole history of the world in the twentieth century, was the Russian revolution of 1917. After a Bolshevik victory in the civil war, the USSR burst onto the world stage as the first Marxist state ever, officially atheistic, doctrinally anti-Christian and based on a materialistic view of man and of life.

3. The inter-war years practically coincided with the pontificate of Pius XI. It was quite a well-defined period of Christianity. The prestige of the Holy See grew enormously and its international personality was strengthened by the signing of many concordats, some with countries created after the first world war. Shortly after 1918 relations between France and the Holy See were normalized (not that there would be no further trouble in the future). But the main event in the area of relations between the Holy See and states was the signing of the Lateran treaty, which brought the Roman question to an end. The realism of Benito Mussolini, the head of the Italian government, and the good will of Pius XI, managed to solve this problem once and for all, to the relief of the very many who were both Italian patriots and faithful Catholics. The agreement, signed on 11 February 1929, created the Vatican City State, the minimum territory necessary for ensuring the independence of the Holy See. It also included a concordat which, like that made in 1933 with Hitler's Germany, survived the disappearance, in the second world war, of the political régime which subscribed to it.

4. There were other good signs. The missions in Asia and Africa made great progress; there were many conversions and the new Christian communities were maturing fast: a good indication of this was the growth of a native clergy which steadily took over from missionaries. An important date in the history of the missions was 28 October 1926, when Pius XI ordained six Chinese bishops in St Peter's.

5. The inter-war years were the hey-day of Catholic Action. Pius XI gave great importance to the lay apostolate and strove to fit it inside a revamped Catholic Action. As a multi-form apostolic movement Catholic Action had been in existence for some time and had been keenly supported by St Pius X. Pius XI now gave it a centralized and hierarchical structure, with a view to its acting as a Christianizing influence in a society which was becoming more and more secularized. He conceived Catholic Action as 'the participation of the organized laity in the hierarchical apostolate of the Church . . . to bring about the universal kingdom of Christ.'

The institution of the feast of Christ the King in the encyclical *Quas primas* (1925) was an expression of this ideal of the social kingship of Jesus Christ, a core element in Pius XI's teaching. His encyclical on marriage *Casti connubii* (30 December 1930) and *Quadragesimo anno* (15 May 1931), updating church teaching on social matters, must both be seen in this light.

6. Although this was a period of great Christian development, a whole wave of bloody persecution affected the Church in a number of countries. In Russia, the implantation of communism led to all sorts of anti-religious violence, affecting mainly the Orthodox Church. But even countries with catholic majorities saw persecutions far worse than that produced by the anticlericalism of the nineteenth century: what happened in Mexico and especially in Spain during its civil war (1936-9) was on a scale unheard of before in modern times. The seven thousand Spanish priests liquidated out of hatred of religion — that is, for the simple fact of being priests — fill an unforgettable page of Christian history, independent of the political rights and wrongs of the Spanish situation.

7. In the third decade of the century the threat from pagan or atheist totalitarianism grew ever greater. Two documents of Pius XI's magisterium show quite clearly what the catholic Church's attitude was to the great totalitarian ideologies of the time — in March 1937 the encyclical *Mit brennender Sorge*, against national socialism and its racist doctrines, and, a few days later, *Divini Redemptoris*, which condemned atheistic Marxism, the official creed of communist Russia. These two totalitarianisms brought the world to the second world war, whose outcome still painfully affects the Christian destinies of people in our own time.

34

The Politico-Religious Consequences
of the Second World War

The second world war caused immense suffering, which continued into the post-war period. Its concentration camps and forced migration of millions of families are without precedent in modern times. After the defeat of fascist totalitarianism, a large part of Europe found itself controlled by another totalitarianism, with an atheistic ideology, which greatly restricted the freedom of Christians. The implantation of communist regimes in China and other countries prevented missionary activity from continuing; while the Church developed further in the Third World countries free from Marxist control.

1. The second world war (1939-45) lasted longer and was on a greater scale than the first. It extended from one end of the globe to the other, and advances in technology increased the destructive power of armaments and caused millions of deaths. And far from the battlefields, millions more lost their lives in aerial bombardments or underwent tremendous suffering and death in concentration camps or the forced labour camps invented by the totalitarian régimes, a phenomenon without precedent in countries with a Christian civilization.

2. Peace did not bring the sufferings of civil populations to an end — particularly in central Europe. The new political frontiers and the division of the old continent into zones of influence obliged huge numbers of families to leave their homelands and to emigrate, penniless, in search of a new country which would take them in. Migration within Europe or from Europe to America reached a scale never before known: one would have to go back to the barbarian invasions to find anything like it — but with this difference: that the barbarians migrated of their own free will.

3. The fascist totalitarian régimes were defeated in the second world war; but communist totalitarianism was not: due to a curious inversion of the original line-up of the conflict, the USSR, from 1941, fought on the side which won — that of the western democracies. The partition of the world agreed on at Yalta by the Allied leaders meant that half of eastern Europe was placed under the control of the Soviet Union. The result was, very soon, communist régimes were forcibly imposed on a number of European countries, while others — this happened to the Baltic countries — simply ceased to exist as nations, being integrated into the USSR as constituent republics. Eastern Europe after world war two was a land without liberty where Christianity and the Church lived in a state of oppression. Cardinals Mindszenty, Stepinac, Wysziński and Tomasek symbolized in the modern world the heroism of the great defenders of the faith.

4. The spread of communism also affected Asia and Africa. In China, where Christianity had been flourishing, Catholics were forbidden all communication with the Holy See and a schismatic church was imposed on them. Other Marxist states placed similar obstacles in the way of freedom of action of the catholic Church. But Christianity experienced a huge growth in the countries of the Third World, free from Marxist control. A native episcopacy and native clergy is now the rule in most of the new countries and this has meant that the inevitable tensions created by the de-colonization process did not adversely effect the catholic Church: it is regarded by the peoples of these countries as being theirs and not something foreign.

5. This advance towards greater real universality of the Church was particularly noticeable during Pius XII's pontificate (2 March 1939 - 9 October 1958). Pius took a particularly important step when in 1946 he made his first appointments of cardinals. Since his election, and due to the war, he had not appointed a single new cardinal; now there were thirty-five vacancies in a college of cardinals which then had seventy places. In his first appointments Pius XII created four Italian cardinals, and twenty-eight from other countries, thus bringing to an end a period of centuries during which Italians had always been in an absolute majority in the sacred college.

6. Pius XII was an indefatigable teacher; in his many addresses he dealt with all aspects of Christian life and morality in the new circumstances of the world. From the doctrinal point of view his encyclical *Humani generis* (12 August 1950) was particularly interesting; it echoed the teaching of St Pius X at a time when the first symptoms of neo-Modernism were beginning to be noticed. Pius

XII was succeeded by John XXIII (28 October 1958 - June 1963), whose pontificate, though short, was important: within three months of his election, on the feast of the conversion of St Paul, 1959, he announced his intention of holding an ecumenical council. On 25 December 1961 the bull *Humanae salutis* officially convoked the second Vatican council.

35

Christianity in the Last Years
of the Twentieth Century

In its documents the second Vatican council outlined an important programme for Christian renewal, which has nothing to do with the abuses committed in the name of a so-called 'conciliar spirit.' The world today suffers from a deep crisis in spiritual values, partly due to the consumer society's demands for higher standards of living, the loss of the supernatural meaning of life, and a trend which sees Christianity and the Church as having a primordially earthly role. The Church has to be, at this time, the defender of such essential values as the right to life, the dignity of the human person and the unity of the family. In the human society at the end of the twentieth century, the Church looks — as it looked in its very earliest times — like the religion of the disciples of Jesus Christ who, with the help of grace, strive to respond to the calling they have received from him.

1. 'To foster the spread of the catholic faith and a healthy renewal of the customs of the Christian people, and to adapt church discipline to the circumstances of our time': these were, in the words of the bull of convocation, the goals the second Vatican council would pursue. Opened by John XXIII on 11 October 1962, only the first sessions were held in the lifetime of this pope. His successor, Paul VI (21 June 1963 - 6 August 1978), governed the Church during the three later stages held in the following three years, up to the closure of the council on 8 December 1965. The council did an enormous amount of work on a wide range of documents — dogmatic constitutions, decrees, declarations and a pastoral constitution on the Church in the modern world. The second Vatican council did not make any dogmatic definitions, so therefore its decrees do not have the prerogative of infallibility; but they do form acts of the solemn magisterium of the Church and they require external and internal obedience of the faithful.

2. The council outlined an important programme for Christian renewal, which can bring great good to the Church. But the period within which it was held also witnessed the effects of a deep crisis in ecclesiastical life which took the form of abuses committed in the name of what was claimed to be 'the spirit of the council' but which had nothing to do with the genuine spirit of the council or with the letter of its documents. Without going into details about the recent past, it may be said that there was a violent neo-modernist explosion in the life of the Church, not limited as earlier Modernism was to a relatively few clerical sectors in Europe, but affecting almost the whole world. An eclipse of the theological virtue of faith and a loss of the eternal meaning of man's life seem to be at the root of this crisis, which tends to distort the nature of redemption and, therefore, of the Church's mission in the world. For neo-modernist innovators, the redemption does not have as its main purpose the eternal salvation of man, by breaking the bonds of sin, but rather the liberation of mankind from earthly oppressions and enslavements. Therefore, the Church's primary role is in the temporal sphere — to fight against the unjust structures of society and the inequalities which exist among people and nations and social classes (this is the basic thesis of 'liberation theology').

3. In the so-called 'free world', economic development after the second world war has seen the growth in the richer countries of a new consumer society which has shown a remarkable capacity to undermine the Christian spirit. The thrill of consumerism has sent a wave of practical materialism over people in all levels of society, a pleasure-seeking urge to enjoy earthly things in an unlimited way, forgetting all about eternal realities — in other words a materialistic view of human life, which sees nothing further than this present life. Among the more characteristic expressions of this phenomenon are a decrease in religious practice in traditionally Christian countries; many marriages in crisis and a crisis in the very institution of the family, with it becoming more and more the victim of divorce; attacks on the right to life of the more defenceless; and increasing violence in society.

The supreme magisterium of the Church has untiringly proclaimed catholic teaching in all its integrity. Among the more important documents of Paul VI special mention should be made of his encyclical *Humanae vitae* (25 July 1968) on problems of marriage and the family, and the 'Credo' of the people of God (30 June 1968), where the basic propositions of the catholic faith are re-stated, with special emphasis on those truths which recent errors have tended to cloud.

4. But in the ups and downs of these new times, the Holy Spirit continues to direct the history of mankind, which will end with the second coming of Jesus Christ. A clear instance of this action of the Spirit who renews the face of the earth of the birth of Opus Dei, a remarkable pastoral and ascetical phenomenon raised up by God to serve the Church and contribute to the eternal and temporal good of mankind. Opus Dei was founded by Blessed Josemaria Escrivá de Balaguer on 2 October 1928. Today it is to be found on all five continents. The universal call to holiness and personal sanctification through ordinary work form the core of Opus Dei's message; and this good news of the universality of the Christian vocation, which so surprised many people when its founder was spreading his message, has become, after Vatican II, part of the general teaching of the catholic Church. Precisely in application of the conciliar documents, the Holy See established Opus Dei as a personal prelature (28 November 1982).

5. In the closing years of the twentieth century, Christianity is reasserting its universality more and more. Today the majority of Catholics are not to be found in the old Europe and North America but in the young nations of the Third World. To the astonishment of all, there occurred on 16 October 1978 an event of enormous significance: following on the brief pontificate of John Paul I, Cardinal Wojtyla, archbishop of Cracow, was elected pope. For the first time in over four and a half centuries, the new pope was not an Italian; for the first time in the history of the Church a Slav, John Paul II, occupied the See of Peter. This historic event has had immense consequences, easy to discern now that he held his office for almost fifteen years. Starting in 1989 a dramatic series of developments (impossible to foresee even a few years earlier) led to the collapse of the communist regimes of Eastern Europe, and the citizens of those nations (and of all the countries which made up the Soviet Union) have begun in fact and in law to enjoy religious freedom. That extensive part of Christian Europe can now look to the future with immense hope, despite the serious economic problems it is experiencing. John Paul II has played a leading role in this great process of liberation; moreover, his 'care for all the churches' has led him to undertake countless pastoral journeys to the five continents, proclaiming the Gospel message to all the peoples of the contemporary world.

6. The catholic Church – towards which all Christians and all men of good will look in hope – is like that lamp described in the Gospel, set on high, spreading its light of Truth and fulfilling the mission of salvation given it by its divine Founder. Now that freedom has returned to many places where Christians of this century underwent persecution, the Church has to meet new challenges from other enemies already mentioned – practical materialism, hedonism, and the pursuit of material well-being as the supreme goal of life. The Church today is seen as the great defender of human life, of man's dignity as a son of God, of human freedom, and of marriage and the family. In the world as it approaches the twenty-first century, Christianity looks – as it looked in its very earliest years – like the religion of the disciples of Jesus Christ who, with the help of grace, strive to respond to their Christian vocation and to spend their life faithfully following their Lord and Master.

Chronological Table

Dates	Events

1st century

Dates	Events
8-4 B.C.	Birth of Christ.
14 A.D.	Death of Augustus.
14-37	Tiberius, emperor.
April 30	Passion, death and resurrection of Jesus Christ.
34	Martyrdom of St Stephen.
34	Conversion of St Paul.
44	Martyrdom of Apostle James the Greater.
c. 50	Council of Jerusalem.
54-68	Nero, emperor.
58	Imprisonment of St Paul in Jerusalem.
58-60	St Paul's captivity in Caesarea.
61-3	St Paul's captivity and release in Rome.
63-5	St Paul's last apostolic journey to Spain and the east.
64	Burning of Rome, persecution of the Christians and probable martyrdom of St Peter.
66-7	Second trial and martyrdom of St Paul in Rome.
70	Siege and destruction of Jerusalem by Titus.
95	Domitian's persecution; St John, exiled on the island of Patmos, writes the Apocalypse.
98-100	St John, the last Apostle, dies in Ephesus.

2nd century

Dates	Events
98-117	Trajan, emperor.
110(?)	Martyrdom in Rome of St Ignatius of Antioch.
117-38	Hadrian, emperor.
140	The beginning of the crisis of Christian Gnosticism.
138-61	Antoninus Pius, emperor.
155(?)	Martyrdom of St Polycarp, disciple of St John.
161-80	Marcus Aurelius, emperor.
180(?)	Foundation of the catechetical school of Alexandria.
c. 185	St Irenaeus' *Against Heresies*.
193-211	Septimus Severus, emperor.
197	Tertullian's *Apology*.

3rd century

203	Origen begins to direct the school of Alexandria.
212	Caracalla grants Roman citizenship to all inhabitants of the empire, with the exception of *dediticii*, people who had surrendered unconditionally.
222-35	Alexander Severus, emperor.
c. 232	Origen, expelled from Alexandria, founds the school of Caesarea in Palestine.
235-84	The period of 'military anarchy' in the Roman empire.
250	Decius' persecution: the *lapsi*.
257-9	Valerian's persecution: the martyrdom of Pope Sixtus II and Lawrence the Deacon, in Rome; and of Bishop Cyprian of Carthage and Bishop Fructuosus of Tarragona.
284-305	Diocletian, emperor: the tetrarchy.

4th century

303-05	The great persecution by Diocletian.
306-37	Constantine, emperor (total sovereignty from 324).
311	Galerius' edict of toleration of Christians.
313	Edict of Milan granting religious freedom.
325	The first council of Nicaea (first ecumenical council) condemns Arianism.
328-73	Athanasius, bishop of Alexandria.
330	Constantinople, the new capital of the empire.
337-79	Pro-Arian emperors, successors of Constantine.
378-95	Theodosius, emperor.
380-400	Conversion of the Visigoths and other Germanic peoples to Arianism.
381	First council of Constantinople (second ecumenical).
395	Arcadius and Honorius, emperors: division of the empire into east and west.
397	Death of St Ambrose, bishop of Milan.

5th century

406	The barbarians cross the Rhine and invade Gaul.
413-27	St Augustine writes *The City of God*.
419-507	Tolosanian Visogoth kingdom in Gaul and Iberia.
420	Death of St Jerome, in Bethlehem.
430	Death of St Augustine, in Hippo.
431	Council of Ephesus (third ecumenical): definition of Mary's divine maternity, and condemnation of Nestorius.
440-61	Pontificate of St Leo I, the Great.
451	Council of Chalcedon (fourth ecumenical): definition of the two natures of Christ and condemnation of Monophysitism
457/61	Death of St Patrick: Ireland, Christian.
493	Ostrogoth kingdom of Italy.
497-8	Baptism of Clovis and conversion of the Franks to Christianity.

6th century

507	Victory of the Franks over the Visigoths: the end of the Tolosanian kingdom.
527-65	Justinian, emperor of the east.
535-54	Gothic war in Italy.
547	Death of St Benedict.
553	Second council of Constantinople (fifth ecumenical): the condemnation of the Three Chapters.
560-570	The conversion to Catholicism of the Suevian kingdom of Galicia: St Martin of Braga.
568-774	The Lombard kingdom of Italy.
589	The third council of Toledo: conversion of the Visigoths to Catholicism.
590-604	Pontificate of St Gregory the Great.
597	Start of the evangelization of Anglo-Saxon England.

7th century

610-41	Heraclius, emperor of the East.
622	The *Hegira*, the beginning of the Islamic era
632	Death of Muhammad.
633-702	The fourth to the eighteenth councils of Toledo.
638	Jerusalem taken by the Arabs.
642	Alexandria taken by the Arabs.
680-81	Third council of Constantinople (sixth ecumenical): doctrine of the two wills of Christ and condemnation of monothelitism.
698	Carthage taken by the Arabs.

8th century

711-12	Conquest of Spain by the Arabs; destruction of the Visigoth kingdom.
717-18	Leo III the Syrian defeats the Arabs at Constantinople and saves the Byzantine empire.
726-80	First period of iconoclasm.
732	Victory of Charles Martel over the Arabs in Poitiers.
751	Start of the Carolingian monarchy in France.
752-7	Beginning of the states of the Church.
754	Martyrdom of St Boniface, apostle of Germany.
768-814	Kingdom of Charlemagne.
774	Suppression of the Lombard kingdom in Italy.
787	Second council of Nicaea (seventh ecumenical): doctrine about the veneration of sacred images.
800	Charlemagne is crowned emperor in Rome.

9th century

815-43	Second period of iconoclasm.
814-40	Reign of Louis the Pious.
840-77	Reign of Charles the Bald.
843	Treaty of Verdun: division of the Carolingian empire.

847-86	Patriarchs Ignatius and Photius twice in sequence occupy the see of Constantinople.
858-67	Pontificate of Nicholas I.
863-85	Missionary work of St Cyril (+ 869) and Methodius.
864	Baptism of Prince Boris and the Bulgar problem
869-70	Fourth council of Constantinople (eighth ecumenical).
891-96	Pope Formosus: state of the Iron Age of the papacy.

10th century

904-54	Rome dominated by the Tusculani family.
909	Foundation of Cluny monastery.
929	Martyrdom of St Wenceslaus, duke of Bohemia.
936-73	Otto I, king of Germany.
962	Otto I crowned by Pope John XII: restoration of the western Christian empire.
966	Baptism of Prince Mieszko and conversion of Poland.
985	Baptism of Gézo, duke of the Hungarians.
988	Baptism of Prince Vladimir and Christianization of Russia.
1000	St Stephen, crowned king of Hungary.

11th century

1002	Death of Emperor Otto III; a new period of Iron Age of the papacy.
1039-56	Henry III, German emperor, takes control of papal elections.
1046-57	The German popes, forerunners of the Gregorian reform.
1054	Michael Cerularius, patriarch of Constantinople: start of the eastern schism.
1056-1106	Henry IV, German emperor.
1073-85	Pontificate of St Gregory VII, which gives its name to the Gregorian reform.
c. 1075	The investiture struggle begins.
1095	In Clermont Urban II preaches the first crusade.
1099	The crusaders take Jerusalem.

12th century

1115-53	St Bernard, abbot of Clairvaux.
1119	Foundation of the Templars.
c. 1120	The Hospitallers become a military order.
1122	Concordat of Worms: the end of the investiture struggle.
1123	First council of the Lateran (ninth ecumenical).
1139	Second council of the Lateran (tenth ecumenical).
c. 1140	*Decretum* of Gratian.
1152-90	Frederick Barbarossa, emperor.
1159-81	Pontificate of Alexander III.
1159(?)	Peter Lombard's *Book of Sentences*.
1179	Third council of the Lateran (eleventh ecumenical).
1187	Jerusalem falls again into Islamic hands.
1198-1216	Pontificate of Innocent III.

13th century

1204	Fourth crusade: Constantinople is taken and a Latin empire is created.
1209-29	Crusade against the Albigenses.
1215	Fourth council of the Lateran (twelfth ecumenical).
1215	Innocent III gives papal sanction to the University of Paris.
1216	Honorius III approves the Order of Preachers (Dominicans).
1223	Solemn approval by Honorius III of the Franciscan order.
1226	Death of St Francis of Assisi.
1226-70	St Louis, king of France.
1229	Frederick II Hohenstaufen (1220-50) regains Jerusalem.
1234	The *Decretales* of Gregory IX.
1244	Jerusalem is finally lost.
1245	First council of Lyons (thirteenth ecumenical).
1261	The end of the Latin empire of Constantinople.
1266-73	St Thomas Aquinas writes the *Summa Theologiae*.
1274	Second council of Lyons (fourteenth ecumenical).
1285-1314	Philip the Fair, king of France.
1294-1303	Pontificate of Boniface VIII.

14th century

1309	The popes establish themselves at Avignon.
1311-12	Council of Vienne (fifteenth ecumenical): the Templars are suppressed.
1324	Marsilius of Padua publishes his *Defensor pacis*.
1347-53	The Black Death.
1347	Death of William of Ockham.
1377	Pope Gregory XI returns from Avignon to Rome.
1378-1417	The western schism: Christendom divided into two obediences.
1382	Condemnation of Wyclif.

15th century

1409	Council of Pisa: election of a third pope.
1414-18	Council of Constance (sixteenth ecumenical).
1415	Death of John Huss at the stake.
1417	The end of the western schism: Martin V, the only pope.
1431-49	Council of Basle-Ferrara-Florence (seventeenth ecumenical).
1439	Union of the Greeks with the catholic Church at the Council of Florence.
1453	Constantinople falls to the Turks: the end of the Christian empire of the east.
c. 1455	Invention of printing.
1474-1516	Reign of the catholic monarchs Isabella (+ 1504) and Ferdinand.
1492	The end of the Spanish reconquest and the discovery of America.

16th century

1509-47	Henry VIII, king of England.
1512-17	Fifth council of the Lateran (eighteenth ecumenical).
1515-47	Francis I, king of France.
1516-56	Charles I of Spain and (from 1519) V of Germany.
1517	Start of the Lutheran revolt.
1520	Excommunication of Luther.
1524	Foundation of the Theatines.
1530	The Confession of Augsburg, composed by Melanchthon.
1533	The English schism.
1536	Death of Erasmus of Rotterdam.
1537	Foundation of the Society of Jesus.
1538	Foundation of the University of Santo Domingo, the first in the new world.
1541-64	Calvin's theocratic government of Geneva.
1545-63	Council of Trent (nineteenth ecumenical).
1546	Death of Luther.
1555	The peace of Augsburg sanctions religious division in Germany.
1556-98	Philip II, king of Spain.
1558-1603	Elizabeth I consolidates the reformation of England.
1562-98	Wars of religion in France.
1566-72	Pontificate of St Pius V.
1571	Battle of Lepanto.
1582	Death of St Teresa of Jesus.
1595	Death of St Philip Neri.
1598	Henry IV of France guarantees toleration to the Huguenots (edict of Nantes).

17th century

1618-48	The Thirty Years War.
1620	The Pilgrim Fathers arrive in America.
1622	Death of St Francis de Sales.
1624-42	Richelieu's government of France.
1633	Trial of Galileo.
1643-1715	Louis XIV, king of France.
1648	The treaty of Westphalia confirms the religious division of Europe.
1649-58	Cromwell in power in England.
1653-1713	The Jansenist crisis — from the condemnation of the five propositions to the bull *Unigenitus Dei filius*.
1660-89	The Stuart restoration in England and Ireland: Charles II and James II.
1682	Gallicanism: the four Organic Articles.
1682-1725	Peter the Great, czar of Russia.
1683	John III Sobieski, king of Poland, defeats the Turks and saves Vienna.
1685	Revocation of the edict of Nantes.
1688-9	The 'glorious revolution' in England: William of Orange, William III.

18th century

1702-13	The war of the Spanish succession.
1715-74	Louis XV, king of France.
1738	Pope Clement XII condemns Freemasonry.
1740-58	Pontificate of Benedict XIV.
1740-80	Maria Theresa, ruler of Habsburg dominions.
1740-86	Frederick II, king of Prussia.
1751-72	Publication of the *Encyclopédie*.
1762-96	Catherine II, empress of Russia.
1765-90	Joseph II of Austria: Josephinism.
1772-95	The first, second and third partitions of Poland.
1773	Pope Clement XIV suppresses the Society of Jesus.
1776	Declaration of independence of the United States of America.
1778	Death of Voltaire and Rousseau.
1781	Kant publishes his *Critique of Pure Reason*.
1786	Absolutism: the synod of Pistoia.
1789	Start of the French revolution.
1790	The 'civil constitution of the clergy.'
1792-4	Abolition of the monarchy in France; execution of Louis XVI; the Terror.
1799	Pope Pius VI (1775-99) dies a prisoner in France.
1800-23	Pontificate of Pius VII.
1799-1804	Napoleon, first consul.

19th century

1801	Concordat between the Holy See and France.
1804-14	The Napoleonic empire.
1810-25	Spanish colonies on the continent of south and central America gain independence.
1814-15	The congress of Vienna and the Holy Alliance.
1814-30	Restoration of the Bourbons in France.
1829	Roman Catholic Relief Act, in United Kingdom — 'Catholic emancipation' — won by Daniel O'Connell.
1830	The July revolutions: Louis-Philippe, king of the French (1830-48); Belgium becomes independent of Holland.
1831-46	Pontificate of Gregory XVI.
1832	Encyclical *Mirari vos* against liberalism.
1837-1901	Victoria, queen of the United Kingdom.
1833-45	The Oxford movement: conversion of Newman to Catholicism (1845).
1846-78	Pontificate of Pius IX.
1848	The revolution of 1848. The exile of Pius IX. Karl Marx publishes the *Communist Manifesto*.
1848-1916	Francis Joseph I, emperor of Austria.
1849	The Roman republic.
1852-70	Second French empire: Napoleon III.
1859	Foundation of the Salesians by St John Bosco.
1864	The 'Syllabus of Errors.'

1869-70	First council of the Vatican (twentieth ecumenical): definition of papal infallibility.
1870	Rome captured and becomes capital of the kingdom of Italy. The end of the papal states.
1870-71	Franco-Prussian war: the new German empire.
1871-79	The *Kulturkampf* in Germany.
1878-1903	Pontificate of Leo XIII.
1880-82	Secularization of French education system.
1883	Death of Karl Marx.
1888-1918	Kaiser William II.
1891	Encyclical *Rerum novarum*, on the social question.

20th century

1903-14	Pontificate of St Pius X.
c. 1903-07	Modernism and its condemnation.
1904-05	France breaks with the Holy See; Church and state are separated.
1914-18	First world war.
1914-22	Pontificate of Benedict XV.
1917	Russian revolution: Lenin.
1919	Treaty of Versailles: a new map of Europe.
1922-39	Pontificate of Pius XI.
1922-43	Fascism in Italy: Mussolini.
1928	Foundation of Opus Dei.
1929	The Lateran treaty brings the Roman question to an end.
1937	Encyclicals condemning racist national socialism and atheistic communism.
1939-45	Second world war: defeat of fascist régimes and subsequent division of the world into two, the western democracies and the communist block.
1939-58	Pontificate of Pius XII.
1949	The People's Republic of China.
1958-63	Pontificate of John XXIII.
1960	High point of decolonialization process in Africa.
1962-65	Second council of the Vatican (twenty-first ecumenical).
1963-78	Pontificate of Paul VI.
1978	Pontificate of John Paul I (26 August - 28 September).
1978	Start of Pontificate of John Paul II (16 October).

Index

My Angel will go Before You

GEORGES HUBER

Do angels exist? Are they not just a pious fiction invented to please children — like Father Christmas? In this era of atomic energy does it make sense to seek the help of the guardian angels?

Angels do exist, is the answer Georges Huber gives as he explores the experience of recent popes, the teaching of Vatican II, the evidence in the Bible and the Liturgy and the writings of saints and masters of the spiritual life. After discussing the difficulties Christians today have in relating to angels, he describes the various ways in which they play an effective and subtle part in people's everyday lives. He shows how familiarity with the angels counters the feelings of loneliness and anguish which 'depth psychology' identifies.

Character Building:

A Guide for Parents and Teachers

DAVID ISAACS

In this book, David Isaacs, an educationalist and parent, offers ideas and suggestions on how parents and teachers can help children's all-round development.

The emphasis in on *character building*, approached from the viewpoint of moral habits: Professor Isaacs takes twenty four virtues and discusses how the child — at different ages — can be encouraged to be obedient, industrious, sincere, prudent, generous, optimistic, sociable and so forth.

The Navarre Bible: New Testament

This twelve-volume series consists of the following elements:

- Revised Standard Version Catholic edition
- New Vulgate; Latin text of New Testament
- Commentaries and Introductions to the books of the New Testament.

The commentaries provide explanations of the doctrinal and practical meaning of the scriptural text, drawing on a rich variety of sources, Church documents, the exegesis of Fathers and Doctors, and the works of prominent spiritual writers, particularly Blessed J. Escrivá, who initiated the Navarre Bible project.

REVIEWS

'We heartily and strongly recommend this splendid volume [St Mark]. It is just what so many have been waiting for' Wm. G. Most, *Homiletic & Pastoral Review*.

'This [Acts] is a superb volume for adult Bible study as well as college and university work; most helpful, enlightening and fascinating' David Liptak, *Catholic Transcript,* Hartford, Conn.

'What I find most useful in this edition is its attitude to Scripture. The Gospels are presented unambiguously as the inspired Word of God and, with the help of the commentaries, we are introduced to two thousand years of contemplative Christian reading and living of the sacred word. This edition is both prayerful and, in the true sense of the word, scholarly' Andrew Byrne, *Osservatore Romano* (English edition).

'It has appeal for the specialist as well as general readership, as much of the commentary consists of a selection of the most interesting observations from two thousand years of scholarship' *Catholic Weekly,* N.S.W.

'It is refreshing to come across a non-technical commentary which ... seeks to expound the Word of God according to the accumulated wisdom of the Church. Most people desiring to understand better the Scriptures are looking for something that will deepen their reverence for the Word of God, help them apply it to their daily lives, and move them to prayer' *Faith Magazine*.

The Navarre Bible: twelve single volumes

*St Matthew   St Mark   St Luke   St John   Acts of the Apostles
Romans & Galatians   Thessalonians & Pastoral Epistles
Captivity Epistles   Corinthians   Hebrews   Catholic Epistles   Revelation*